THE MORAL POWER OF MONEY

CULTURE AND ECONOMIC LIFE

THE MORAL POWER OF MONEY

Morality and Economy in the Life of the Poor

ARIEL WILKIS

STANFORD UNIVERSITY PRESS
STANFORD, CALIFORNIA

Stanford University Press
Stanford, California

This work is published within the framework of the "Sur" Translation Support Program of the Ministry of Foreign Affairs, International Trade and Worship of the Argentine Republic. Obra editada en el marco del Programa "Sur" de Apoyo a las Traducciones del Ministerio de Relaciones Exteriores, Comercio Internacional y Culto de la República Argentina.

A version of this book was originally published in Spanish in 2013 under the title *Las sospechas del dinero. Moral y economía en el mundo popular* © 2013, Paidos—Buenos Aires.

Printed in the United States of America on acid-free, archival-quality paper

Library of Congress Cataloging-in-Publication Data

Names: Wilkis, Ariel, author.
Title: The moral power of money : morality and economy in the life of urban poor / Ariel Wilkis. Other titles: Sospechas del dinero.
English Description: Stanford, California : Stanford University Press, 2017. | Series: Culture and economic life | Originally published in 2013 in Spanish under the title: Las sospechas del dinero : moral y economia en el mundo popular. | Includes bibliographical references and index. | Description based on print version record and CIP data provided by publisher; resource not viewed.
Identifiers: LCCN 2017015911 (print) | LCCN 2017021410 (ebook) | ISBN 9781503604360 () | ISBN 9781503602861 (cloth : alk. paper) | ISBN 9781503604285 (pbk. : alk. paper)
Subjects: LCSH: Poor—Argentina—Buenos Aires. | Money—Moral and ethical aspects—Argentina—Buenos Aires. | Money—Social aspects—Argentina—Buenos Aires. | Buenos Aires (Argentina)—Social conditions.
Classification: LCC HV4070.B84 (ebook) | LCC HV4070.B84 W55 2017 (print) | DDC 339.4/60982—dc23
LC record available at hgps://lccn.loc.gov/2017015911

To my parents, Ricardo and Silvia Wilkis

Contents

Acknowledgments

This is a fully revised translation of my book *Las sospechas del dinero. Moral y economía en el mundo popular* (Buenos Aires: Paidos, 2013). Several people and organizations were supportive during my rewriting of it for almost three years. First, I would like to thank Argentina's Consejo Nacional de Investigaciones Cientificas y Tecnológicas (CONICET; the National Council of Science and Technology Research) and the Instituto de Altos Estudios Sociales at the Universidad Nacional de San Martín; as my employers, both have supported my endeavors as a sociologist. I am extremely grateful to Fred Wherry, co-editor of Stanford University Press's Culture and Economic Life series, for his generous support and encouragement. SUP editors Jenny Gavacs and Kate Wahl were also extremely helpful throughout the process: Jenny at the beginning, and Kate in the final stages. Wendy Gosselin did a formidable job on the translation, and I would like to thank her for embarking with me on this three-year adventure. Viviana Zelizer encouraged me to believe in my work and convinced me that publishing this book was well worthwhile. Several friends and colleagues provided advice and recommendations on negotiating the world of American university presses; among them, I would like to especially thank Daniel Fridman, Martín Sivak, Valeria Manzano, Horacio Ortiz, Máximo Badaro, Nicolas D'Avella, Alejandro Dujovne, Marcela Amador Ospina, and Carlos Forment. The New School invited me to New York as a visiting scholar, giving me the time I needed to finish the manuscript, and Pablo Miguez, Gabriel Kessler, Julian Troksberg, and Jennifer Adair kept me company while I was there, often at the Silvana bar in Harlem.

Finally, I cannot find the words to thank my son, Manuel, for all that he has given me.

THE MORAL POWER OF MONEY

Introduction

Money and Moral Capital

Perhaps behind the coin is God.

—Jorge Luis Borges, "The Zahir"

MARY IS A FIFTY-EIGHT-YEAR-OLD WOMAN who lives in Villa Olimpia, a *villa miseria* (slum) in greater Buenos Aires, west of the country's capital city. The first slums in Buenos Aires—neglected areas to which the urban poor have historically been relegated—date back to the 1930s. With each passing decade, they expanded as migrants flooded the city, first from provinces across Argentina and later from other South American countries, particularly Paraguay, Bolivia, and Peru. Like so many of these migrants, Mary and her four children arrived from Paraguay twenty-five years ago.

I met Mary on the side of a road at the beginning of 2008. We were waiting for a bus that would take us to a rally organized by the Peronists, a political party historically associated with Argentina's lower classes.[1] I had gone to Villa Olimpia to examine how neoliberalism was changing the way politics are done among the urban poor in Buenos Aires. For many social scientists, neoliberalism had become the key to understanding the difficult path towards consolidating democracy in countries of the region, where poverty and social exclusion had been climbing since the previous decade. Employing concepts such as political clientelism, researchers were working to understand the political power dynamics unique to this context (O'Donnell 1996; Auyero 2001; Levitsky 2003). I had come to Villa Olimpia with the idea of exploring what role political clientelism played in power relations in

1

the impoverished neighborhoods of the Buenos Aires periphery. However, as I got to know Mary and her family through regular visits, my interest gradually shifted to another aspect of life in this poor neighborhood.

Years after I had finished my research and published *Las sospechas del dinero* (The Suspicions of Money), which summarized my work in Villa Olimpia, an Argentine newspaper sent a reporter to discuss the book with me. When the journalist inquired about the questions that guided my research, I replied, "You could say that I was trying to get to know Peronism through the patronage system and what I discovered was money" (*Página/12*, January 27, 2014). In other words, my interest in political clientelism waned as my fieldwork advanced, and I realized that a sociocultural analysis of money would allow me to understand not only political relations but also other power relations in the world of the poor.

How could an ethnography on power and politics in the world of the poor culminate with the meanings of money? To answer this question, I would like to share two stories from my fieldwork. The first reveals certain aspects of Mary's involvement in the Peronist political network of Villa Olimpia, a network led by a local political boss named Luis Salcedo. The second explores other aspects of Mary's daily life, especially with regard to supporting her family.

At the beginning of May 2008, I took down the following notes:

Mary is ill. A few years ago she found out that she has a tumor. Sometimes the disease takes over and she needs to rest. Her sons and daughter take care of things at home and keep her company. The neighbors know that when Mary does not come with them to see Luis Salcedo, the local political boss, it is because she is not feeling well. She gets paid for her work as an activist, "a political salary," she likes to clarify. In Villa Olimpia, Mary isn't the only one who gets paid for her work to support Salcedo's political career. A lot of local residents receive a political salary, since the higher up the local leader goes, the more people he needs to consolidate this growth. At the same time, the national government pours more money into the neighborhood to ensure that Salcedo and his people continue to voice their support for the administration. For Mary and other residents of the neighborhood involved in paid politics, this political money brings its own uncertainties: it is rarely clear how much they will earn or when they will be paid.

Over time, I learn that every night before going to bed, Mary spends time at the kitchen table poring over the numbers. Behind these careful calculations is a deep but almost impossible desire to balance a budget that always comes up short. She doesn't always need a notebook to do the math: she knows exactly how much money the household needs and how much she and her children are contributing. In a nutshell, the sum of her equations determines how concerned she needs to be at any given time. Mary's moneymaking begins at La Salada, an enormous street market on the bank of El Riachuelo, a river awash with industrial waste and garbage. At La Salada, she buys clothes at a low price and then resells them. Not all of the earning schemes in Mary's household are licit, however. When her sons come home from the meat-processing factory where they work, they take several pounds of stolen beef out of their bags. Before changing out of their blood-stained clothes, they package the meat in smaller portions; the clients begin ringing the bell shortly after they finish. They negotiate the price for each chunk. Money and meat are exchanged in front of Mary's attentive eyes. Once the meat has been sold, she demands that her sons share the proceeds. "They know they have to give me the money because I do my part!" she says to me, first in Guaraní, an indigenous language, and then in Spanish. Mary imposes this principle not only on the earned money that comes from the stolen beef, but also on the salaries her sons earn. Mary believes that money must be safeguarded to ensure her family can meet its needs.

These seemingly minor details from the lives of Mary and her family show the critical importance of money. There was never enough money, according to Mary, and it was so hard to earn: imagine how many problems could be solved if there were only more of it. In these narratives, the tensions and dilemmas in Mary's dealings with the local political boss and with her children are all overshadowed by the lack of money. Yet these accounts also reveal that money is present in other not-so-obvious ways.

When her *political* money wasn't delivered on time, Mary would get both angry and sad. Depending on how bad she felt, she might discuss the matter with another important neighborhood leader, the local priest. Whenever she sought out Father Suárez for advice, she would inevitably question Salcedo's moral authority. The waiting period was a time reserved for remembering all the promises that the political leader had not followed through on. The priest always gave Mary support, with worldly advice like, "Tell Salcedo to put his money where his mouth is." The recommendation came from someone who knew how to manage money in a context in which material needs, politics, and emotions all came into play. When it came to Mary's children, they were expected to hand over part of the money they *earned* working at the meat market and selling cuts stolen on the job. With this income, Mary was able to just manage the household budget, though depending on the month, there were times when it was difficult to make ends meet. Still, her sons' contribution to the household was about more than money. By obliging them to hand over the money they *earned,* Mary was reaffirming her moral authority, teaching them about masculine responsibility. "That's how they learn to become men," Mary would say as she counted the bills.

Narratives like these reveal that money's existence in the life of the poor is as associated with hardship as it is with the moral dynamics that both define and challenge power relations. In my fieldwork in Villa Olimpia—in households or at political rallies, in the relationships between men and women and between different generations—money had the fundamental ability to sustain, alter, or undermine moral hierarchies. I discovered that the moral dimension of money provided a unique perspective on power relations among the poor, a perspective that eventually led me to write this book. In a dialogue that includes Pierre Bourdieu's sociology of power and Viviana Zelizer's sociology of money, I propose the concept of moral capital to interpret the connections between money, morality, and power.

Classical sociologists like Karl Marx and Georg Simmel depicted modern-day money as a homogeneous and universal device capable of keeping societies united. Sociology later questioned this account of money and substituted another, with myriad uses and meanings, moving away from a stagnant view of it. This new approach provided insight into the way classical authors in the field depicted money and enables us to understand that money is more like a puzzle comprised of several pieces.

I use the figure of the puzzle to build this book's argument. The concept of moral capital allows me to show that the *pieces of money* are shaped by ideas and beliefs about morality, and that each of these pieces differs from the others. The puzzle fits together according to each piece's ability to evaluate, compare, and measure people's virtues.

Erving Goffman (1983) argued that any interaction can be analyzed as a small-scale social order. His sociology showed how people approach and maneuver these different orders, employing them to build their status and ponder their worth as people. In this book, I maintain that the social orders emerging from interactions can be analyzed through pieces of money.

When seen through the lives of Mary and her family, pieces of money are revealed to be diverse, multifaceted and often entwined. I suggest that the following pieces of money that I discovered over the course of my fieldwork establish moral hierarchies among people: *lent* money, *earned* money, *donated* money, *political* money, *sacrificed* money, and *safeguarded money*. I propose that these different pieces are used to create moral hierarchies. The concept of moral capital illuminates this dynamic by showing how people are morally ranked within these hierarchies and power relations are generated as the money circulates. This book thus approaches pieces of money as moral entities, and the money puzzle as a moral puzzle. The dynamic of the pieces—a dynamic involving hierarchies, tensions, and contradictions— challenges the definition and the negotiation of people's status and power in specific social orders.

This book thus expands the sociological model of multiple monies by considering the moral dimension of money as a fundamental part of power relations. The subject of this sociological study, then, is not money but rather the social orders it produces and responds to in the world of the urban poor in greater Buenos Aires.

The World of the Poor Configured in Pieces of Money

Thousands of life stories like those of Mary and her family show how money influences the lives of the poor. Over the past few years, many scholars have focused on money in the world of the poor in both developed countries and the nations in the Global South. Most of the literature concentrates on a single piece of money. However, as I mentioned with regard to Mary and her family, many pieces of money come into play in their lives, but no single one can explain how social life is rooted in money's heterogeneous social and moral dynamics.

First, some of the literature has focused on the piece I refer to as money *earned* to analyze how the poor are involved in the process of globalization. Paul Stoller (2002), for example, sheds light on these connections by examining the use of money among African street sellers in New York City. In Brazil, Rosana Pinheiro Machado (2010) has shown how the money *earned* by street and market sellers in Brazil forges transnational networks that connect Brazil to Paraguay and China. Second, the study of *lent* money has become conducive to analyzing the new dynamics of financialization in the economy of the poor. The forms of capitalism that fostered financial liberalization (Chesnais 2004) have made well-being an individual's personal responsibility. In this context, credit and debt have become core topics in studies of money in the world of the poor. In an extensive volume of articles covering several countries in the Global South (Guérin et al. 2014), financial practices are considered crucial to improving the living conditions of the most underprivileged members of society. Deborah James (2015), for example, reconstructs how black families in South Africa were incorporated into the consumer market after apartheid. This began with a loan market that created new conditions for indebtedness. Finally, other works have focused on *donated* money as a way to understand new forms of social assistance. James Ferguson (2015), for example, discusses the political significance of conditional cash transfers (CCT), which benefit nearly 30 percent of the population of South Africa. Another scholar, Julia Elyachar (2005), analyzed microlending programs among the poor in Egypt to show how they have contributed to a consolidation of neoliberalism. In another take on microlending, Lamia Karim (2011) has examined the exploitation of poor women in Bangladesh by NGOs.

In this literature, money is an insightful way of understanding the relations between macro-social processes and the experiences of the poor. Understanding these dynamics helps us to identify the current conditions for social integration among those who benefit least from neoliberal globalization and financialization. While I acknowledge the contributions of this literature, this book proposes a different approach by simultaneously considering the many pieces of money at work in the social life of neighborhoods like Villa Olimpia. The concept of moral capital is critical to this interpretation.

Money and Development

Scholars were not the only ones to return to the topic of money in the world of the poor. Experts in development have helped create a new paradigm for examining the world of the poor through the looking glass of money, while also expanding on the life stories of people like Mary and her family. *Portfolios of the Poor* (Collins et al. 2009), an acclaimed book that recounts the life stories of women, men, children, and entire families "living on less than two dollars a day," is an excellent example of this new paradigm.[2] These stories are empirically rich, revealing how actors deftly combine multiple financial instruments. In *The Fortune at the Bottom of Pyramid: Eradicating Poverty through Profits* (2005), C. K. Prahalad goes a step further, avoiding the topic of what the poor are lacking and instead focusing on their abilities and, more specifically, their financial capacity. This book describes how many successful businesses in different regions of the Global South incorporate the poor into the world of retail transactions. Prahalad calls on the corporate world to follow their example, since businesses play a critical role in development and in reducing poverty.

Unlike the scholarly literature that I reviewed in the previous section, both *Portfolios of the Poor* and *The Fortune at the Bottom of Pyramid* offer clear-cut guidelines for development. In this paradigm shift away from microfinance, the problem becomes not the poor but the institutional framework that excludes them from the banking system and the formal market. Innovation, then, requires a whole new financial and business system designed to include subaltern groups.

A similar trend is seen among development experts who focus not on NGOs' role in business but on state policies, especially the new CCT programs. These experts also make a case for a paradigm focused on getting money into the hands of the poor, acknowledging their financial abilities and developing the adequate institutional environments to allow low-income individuals to improve their situation. *Just Give Money to the Poor:*

The Development Revolution from the South (Hanlon et al. 2010) analyzes the outcome of programs of this sort in different parts of the world, revealing that beneficiaries use the money "efficiently." The findings of this book also show that CCT programs reduce poverty and in the long term favor economic and social development.

Although this development paradigm provides us with a new perspective on the poor, it offers no such innovation in its approach to money. This is critical to understanding both its scope and the recommendations associated with it. *Portfolios of the Poor, The Fortune at Bottom of Pyramid*, and *Just Give Money to the Poor* do not seek to show how power is built and sustained by money relations; instead, they view power as a contextual variable associated with uses of money. For this reason, their authors are able to propose the idea of expanding financial and market opportunities as strategies to enhance development and overcome poverty without inquiring into the new types of snares these strategies may create for those they intend to benefit. *The Moral Power of Money* takes the opposite path, offering a new perspective on power in the everyday lives of the poor. This conceptual approach begins by exploring the concept of moral capital.

A New Sort of Recognition: Moral Capital

Over the past few years, the sociology of morality has adopted a new agenda, underpinned by the connection between moral dynamics and power relations and shifting away from the search for "normative" components as researchers strive to find new ways to identify moral actions and beliefs (see Hitlin and Vaisey 2010). As Jal Mehta and Christopher Winship observe, connecting morality with power can really get people's attention. Morality and power are often taken to be opposites, with morality grounded in altruism and a commitment to the common good, and power associated with self-interest (Mehta and Winship 2010, 426). Reinterpreting the sociology of Pierre Bourdieu, I seek to show how the concept of moral capital contributes to this new agenda of the sociology of morality by pushing past the simple question of morality versus power.

In the sociology of morality, Bourdieu's work has received little attention. The fact that his sociology has been classified as reproductivist (Merchiers 2004) or utilitarian (Caillé 1994; Alexander 1995) has prevented it from being considered in relation to moral acts. Patrick Pharo has explained this as follows: "If values and virtues are essential [in Bourdieu's work], it is not as objects of knowledge but as tools of political struggle. Ethics remain on the periphery of the system and do not become a direct object of analysis" (Pharo 2004, 124). I believe, however, that certain interpretations of Bourdieu's work have contributed to this oversight.

In his book *Distinction: A Social Critique of the Judgement of Taste*, Bourdieu describes the cultural ethos of the petite bourgeoisie in a way that I believe is highly useful when reflecting on the concept of moral capital:

> The rising petite bourgeoisie endlessly remakes the history of the origins of capitalism; and to do so, like the Puritans, it can only count on its asceticism. In social exchanges, where other people can give real guarantees, money, culture or connections, it can only offer *moral guarantees*; (relatively) poor in economic, cultural and social capital, it can only "justify its pretensions," and get the chance to realize them, by paying in sacrifices, privations, renunciations, goodwill, *recognition*, in short, *virtue*. (Bourdieu 1984, 333; emphasis added)

This paragraph is insightful for many reasons. First of all, Bourdieu argues that moral virtues must be recognized as sustaining a social position; these virtues serve to distinguish the bearer. Second, these virtues can stand in for other types of capital (economic, cultural, and social capital). Respecting individuals—because they have certain values or show goodwill—is the basis for accepting their actions and words as moral guarantees. These moral guarantees stand in for the "real guarantees: money, culture or connections." Here, then, Bourdieu notes that the recognition of virtues can be a source of power.

Bourdieu's sociology deals fundamentally with the legitimacy of power, and this led him to the concept of symbolic capital. Certain interpretations focus on the fact that for Bourdieu, the concept of symbolic capital was based on the central assumption that social life is an endless series of struggles for recognition (Corcuff 2003). However, unlike other approaches by scholars such as Axel Honneth (1996), Bourdieu believed that these struggles are marked by power relations (Bourdieu 2000). Bourdieu's work to develop the concept of symbolic capital created an investigative framework for analyzing the different forms of recognition that confer power and legitimacy. The different subtypes of symbolic capital require different types of recognition. For example, agonistic capital (Mauger 2006) recognizes skill in the use of physical violence. Erotic capital (Hakim 2010) acknowledges adeptness at seduction. In this book, I view the concept of moral capital as another subtype of symbolic capital and, by expanding on Bourdieu's analysis, I argue that it is capable of helping us to understand the dynamic of recognition and its effects on distinguishing individuals based on their perceived morality.

People are constantly measuring, comparing, and evaluating their moral virtues, because these virtues bestow a very specific kind of power. Possessing moral capital means having these virtues acknowledged. Meeting moral obligations, for example, can be a source of such recognition (Mauss 1966), and therefore a source of power as well. The moral component of moral capital thus depends on meeting social obligations in order to have one's virtues acknowledged by others. In this regard, moral capital creates a social ranking: the more of it you have, the more benefits you will reap in a given society.

To illustrate this point, the main ideas of the classic study by Norbert Elias on the dynamics of power between the established and the outsiders in a fictional working-class neighborhood in the 1960s are particularly telling. Elias and John Scotson write: "Approval of group opinions . . . requires compliance with a group's norms. The penalty for group deviance and sometimes even for suspected deviance is loss of power and a lowering of one's status" (Elias and Scotson 1994, 11). These authors focus on the efforts to prove one's morality and thus gain privileged access to power.

As we see in Elias's work, there is an intimate connection between moral capital and the legitimacy of social hierarchies (Dumont 1966). This is a core theme of this book as well. People have certain obligations to meet, and they are ranked accordingly; meeting obligations bestows a social status. Accumulating moral capital means gaining legitimacy in a position on the social hierarchy. The social hierarchies constructed on this subtype of symbolic capital are unstable because they can be challenged and need to be continuously reiterated. The moral universe is not neutral but agonistic, inasmuch as agents vie to stand out from one another. And morality is precisely what allows agonistic and hierarchical positions to unfold in the social realm. While the relationship between morality and power can be explored through Bourdieu's sociology, it is necessary to go beyond his perspective to understand the moral dimension of money. The relationship between money and morality is, according to Bourdieu, between "hostile worlds," to cite Zelizer (2005), and Bourdieu's concept of money is hostile to morality. In both his investigations into the sociogenesis of a capitalist economic habitus among the Algerian peasantry (1977) and in his works on the economic field (2005), Bourdieu tells a one-sided story of money in which it inevitably appears as accidental and separate from morality. Bourdieu tends to view the ever-increasing capitalist money exchanges as dynamics void of the moral values of economic relations. This is the so-called principle of the formation of the "capitalist" economic habitus and of the autonomy of the economic field.

Bourdieu's perspective does not allow the moral dimension of money to be considered in conjunction with an analysis of power relations. His perspective prevents a comprehensive understanding of how money circulates and the resulting moral struggles and power relations. To make this shift, we must go beyond the concept of money presented in Bourdieu's work and move towards the conceptual framework of Zelizer.

From Homogeneity to the Sociology of Multiple Monies

The rebirth of a sociology of money in the 1980s can be interpreted as part of a global trend of questioning money as universal and homogeneous. In the classic narrative, money is viewed as a "general equivalent of value" (Marx 1976 [1867]), "the value of values" (Simmel 1900), or "all-purpose currency" (Polanyi 2001 [1944]). In contrast, a new narrative focused on multiple meanings of money has been constructed in fields like history (Kuroda 2008), economics (Théret 2007), anthropology (Guyer 2012; Neiburg 2016), and sociology (Zelizer 1994; Blanc 2009; Dodd 2014). Unlike the perspective of money as an instrument that can be replaced or exchanged independently of the form it takes (coin, bills, checks, etc.) and of its origins, this new narrative brings up the question of the conditions and limits of its fungibility.

Nigel Dodd (2014) has recently summarized this shift by arguing that while classic sociology focused on how money shapes culture, contemporary sociology does the opposite, revealing how money is formatted by culture. Dodd describes this change as follows:

> Against this [a view of money as culturally corrosive], a strong literature has developed, mainly during the last quarter of the twentieth century, which advances the view that money is richly embedded in and shaped by its social and cultural context. What is needed, according to this view, is a theory of money's *qualities*, not simply an account of its role as a *quantifier*. Such a theory needs to focus not only on how money is "marked" by cultural practices from the outside but also on a deeper level, on the way in which those practices shape money *from within*, for example, by defining its scales of value. (Dodd 2014, 271)

From this point of view, a qualitative theory of money requires the radical belief that culture (or morality) does not influence money from the outside but instead shapes it from the inside. This is about interpreting culture and morality as intrinsic properties of money, not as accidental features that can be ignored when trying to understand how money operates in social life (Bandelj 2012; Wherry 2016). In keeping with this proposal, the challenge is to make the analytical shift from an interpretation of culture or morality as the settings for money practices to a perspective that shows how they produce money from within. In this way, the conceptual refocus that I propose consists of also understanding moral capital as one of money's intrinsic properties. This allows us to combine Bourdieu's perspective on power with Zelizer's concept of multiple monies.

Moral Capital: An Accounting Unit for the Pieces of Money

In *The Social Meaning of Money* (1994), Viviana Zelizer demonstrated that money acts as a powerful socializer. Her sociology offers an inverted image of money in social life in comparison to classical sociologists. While these authors had depicted money as a "social acid" that dissolves interpersonal ties, Zelizer showed how people in fact use money to forge and reinforce such ties, assigning specific transaction types (differentiated ties) and different budgetary earmarks for different types of social ties. Zelizer also emphasized these differences in her concept of the circuits of commerce (2010). The existence and maintenance of these circuits depend on the boundaries established by members of the circuits and others, and the use of relationally marked monies plays a crucial role in establishing such boundaries. More recently, Zelizer proposed the term "relational work" to refer to "creating viable matches among those meaningful relations, transactions, and media" (Zelizer 2012, 151). There is one constant throughout Zelizer's work: money always serves to distinguish (and sometimes condemn) people and their social ties morally.

In light of these analyses, Zelizer's sociology is an invitation to think of money not as payment, exchange, store of value, or abstract accounting unit but as a moral accounting unit. Earlier writers viewed the abstract commensurability of money as its potential to bring people together; Marx, for example, saw the abstraction of money as the basis for people to connect and exchange goods. In this new approach to money, social connections are instead produced through a sort of moral commensurability associated with it. People are measured, assessed, and morally ranked through specific pieces of money in circulation, linking money with the concept of moral capital.

In other words, I suggest that as money circulates, people's moral capital is put to the test. Money allows people to judge the virtues and defects of others and thus establish rankings among the people they know, creating moral hierarchies through money. People can be good for the money; they can be loyal, respectable, generous, and hard-working; or disloyal, unreliable, frivolous, greedy, and lazy (Wherry 2008). These are only some of the classifications that appeared during my research. The moral judgments that people reach reveal how moral capital comes into play when money changes hands or is salted away.

Articulating the concept of moral capital with the sociology of multiple monies involves a conceptual shift with respect to Zelizer's argument. In this shift, I believe the work of the anthropologist Jane Guyer is particularly illuminating. While the sociology of Viviana Zelizer emphasizes the means of payment people choose for intimate transactions, Guyer's anthropology (2004) pays more attention to the hierarchy *between* currencies. In the case studies Zelizer presents, this dimension is much less of a focus. For example, in her book *The Social Meaning of Money*, we know little about the interactions between domestic monies and non-domestic monies, namely, how they are produced and used in market dealings. When we read about the notion of the circuit, we get an in-depth look at how migrants use the money they send back to their country of origin but we find out little about the other monies they use, the monies outside the circuit. In Zelizer's arguments, it is clear these monies are different, but not as clear which take priority over others; as a result, the consideration of how these affect social life is not as insightful as it could be. In contrast, in the context of the economies of Atlantic Africa, Guyer notes how people relate to heterogeneous currencies with different values. In her analysis of economic transactions, people resolve these differences by establishing a hierarchy of payment methods. For Guyer, all monetary transactions express a social order.

In order to analyze the production of moral hierarchies produced by money, I utilize Zelizer's relational perspective and add Guyer's contribution to reveal the hierarchies between currencies. In this framework, to interpret the multiple moral meanings of money I propose replacing Zelizer's notion of "kinds" with "pieces" of money. This analytical shift provides a better framework for understanding the interaction, overlay, and hierarchy of monies.

In the introduction to her recent translation of Marcel Mauss's *The Gift* (2016), Guyer suggests that the original text is like a puzzle that can be assembled in different ways. Instead of offering readers a solid interpretation of the text, Guyer instead helps them put together the puzzle. The puzzle pieces have no established order or outline. Reading *The Gift* thus means discovering these pieces and putting them together in different ways. Guyer's approach to the translation could also apply to my proposal here: I also employ the notion of assembling puzzle pieces, but my aim is to examine the role of money in social life.

The pieces of a puzzle provide only a partial understanding when observed on their own; they need the other pieces to form the big picture. Similarly, the value of each piece depends on how it connects to the others. The move from the notion of "kinds" to "pieces" suggests that moral capital is forged by fitting the different pieces of money together and constructing a pattern. Through these pieces, it is possible to understand how people are judged by certain monetary practices and acquire a certain moral reputation. The money pieces work as moral accounting units, expressing the moral capital that all of the pieces share in the sphere of economic life.

In order to understand the analytical strength of the concept of moral capital, it is important to differentiate it from another important concept that has been used to interpret the relationship between morality and economy. I am referring to the concept of the moral economy. I'll first explain how the concept of moral economy is generally incompatible with a sociology of multiple monies and then explain why the concept of moral capital is better equipped for an analysis of money as a savvy tool for understanding power relations.

Coined by E. P. Thompson, the term "moral economy" emphasizes fairness, justice, and mutuality, values that mobilize opposition to the emerging capitalist economy (Thompson 1971). The concept was later revived in an analysis of resistance to colonial exploitation (Scott 1976). In general terms, Thompson and James Scott both sketch a dichotomy between economies embedded in social activity (the moral economy) versus disembedded economies (i.e., guided by markets), an argument that had a lot in common with Polanyi's work. This argument differs from Zelizer's hypothesis on the moral ubiquity of money. For Zelizer, monetary transactions are always moral negotiations, whether they occur on or off the market. Like other scholars in the field (Boltanski and Thévenot 2006; Stark 2009), Zelizer thus argues that all economies are moral economies, be they embedded or disembedded, calling into question the dichotomy traced by Thompson and Scott.

In place of the moral economy, the concept of moral capital reveals how money can mobilize virtues and moral values according to different monetary logics. We find these monetary and moral dynamics in both the informal and formal economies, in illegal dealings along with those of nongovernmental organizations (NGOs). Paying back what one owes, for example, brings repute on any of these circuits, which can all be interpreted by examining the values that circulate alongside money and the efforts people make to have their virtues acknowledged.

In a more decisive way, the concept of the moral economy collides with a sociology of multiple monies because it does not reveal the relational work of the dominant groups to differentiate themselves. According to Thompson and Scott, the term "moral economy" describes the obligations and norms associated with economic distribution. These moral values encourage subordinated groups to act collectively. From this perspective, the moral economy describes the moral consensuses that allow for resistance to the elites. Thus, it is not a concept that sheds light on the role of money in the moral hierarchy of social groups.

In short, my work here contributes to the literature that has attempted, to cite Marion Fourcade and Kieran Healy (2007), to open up the black box of morality in order to understand how the moral performativity of economy shapes its exchanges and defines legitimate actors. Opening up the black box of morality through the concept of moral capital helps to reveal social dynamics, rules, and behaviors that are often naturalized or otherwise overlooked. This book thus aims at a new way of interpreting the connection between morality and economy, which continues to be a key topic in the social sciences today (Fourcade and Healy 2007; Graeber 2011; Wherry 2012).

Pieces of Money in Context

Pieces of money represent realities that correspond to specific sociohistorical contexts. To paraphrase Marx, we can say that people negotiate their status and power within monetary hierarchies under circumstances not of their choosing. Monetary hierarchies are embedded in institutional and macro-level social dynamics. To briefly summarize the idea, each specific sociohistorical context facilitates the emergence, expansion, and disappearance of certain pieces of money.

At the end of the first decade of the twenty-first century, after nearly thirty years of economic cutbacks, the consequences of neoliberal policies could be felt in the neighborhoods along the periphery of Buenos Aires. These consequences ranged from job market exclusion to a growing informal and illegal economy and severe deterioration of the urban infrastructure. In the years I spent visiting Villa Olimpia, other processes were also under way. When President Nestor Kirchner took office in 2003, Argentina's economic policy took a sudden turn, because his administration questioned neoliberalism and its negative effects among the poorest members of society.[3] This process was continued under President Cristina Fernández de Kirchner, who was elected in 2007. According to political analysts (Cameron and Hershberg 2010; Levitsky and Roberts 2011), these administrations were part of a "left turn" in the first decade of the twenty-first century among the countries of the region (Brazil, Bolivia, Ecuador, Uruguay, and Venezuela). During both of the Kirchner presidencies, the strategy for economic growth was based on expanding consumer spending though different policies, including conditional cash transfers to raise the purchasing power of the lower classes.

The pieces of money that I detected during my fieldwork in Villa Olimpia represent a complex combination of the money dynamics associated with job market exclusion and integration to the consumer market. These dynamics were based on money *earned* from the informal and illegal economy; *lent* money associated with the role of family help and the growing importance of financialization among the poor; *donated* money associated with conditional cash transfers; *political* money that mediated the power relations in democratic governments in contexts of poverty and inequality; *sacrificed* money associated with church and charity work in these same contexts; and money *safeguarded* with family networks that support individuals down on their luck.

The sociohistorical combinations of some of these pieces of money are connected with the neoliberal policies that began to expand globally at the end of the 1970s (Harvey 2005). Based on these processes, there was a "new regime of urban marginality" (Wacquant 2008) in which salaried work began to decline as the principal source of income among dwellers on the urban outskirts, and there was a growing dependence on money from informal and illegal markets, welfare, NGO assistance, and mutual assistance networks among the poor. In Argentina, neoliberal policies were first implemented during the 1976–83 military dictatorship, though such policies were common across the region during the period of authoritarian governments in power during the 1970s and 1980s.

From 1940 until the start of the military dictatorship, Argentina's job market was characterized by formal employment, low levels of unemployment, and a small wage gap (Altimir and Beccaria 1999). During this period, unions provided workers with security and gave them a voice in politics (Torre 1990). Under the military regime, political repression and market deregulation led to lower salaries, a rise in unemployment, and a lack of attention to the poor and the marginalized. Thus, the number of people employed in industry fell by 30 percent between 1974 and 1983 (Schorr 2007). Between 1974 and 1980, the income of contracted salaried workers dropped by 15.5 percent and that of salaried workers without contracts fell by 16.9 percent (FETIA–CTA 2005). While 4.4 percent of the residents of greater Buenos Aires reported incomes placing them below the poverty line in 1974, this had climbed to 11.1 percent by 1980, and by the end of that decade, owing to the effects of hyperinflation, poverty had reached almost half the population (Bayón and Saraví 2002).

During the 1990s, a democratically elected president revived the neoliberal policies initially implemented two decades earlier by the military. Strict measures were needed to stabilize the Argentine economy, and the administration of Carlos Menem (1989–99) opted for neoliberal reforms, including harsh state cutbacks, the privatization of state-owned companies, market deregulation, and the elimination of import tariffs (Torre 1998). One of the most dramatic consequences of these policies was to consolidate the deindustrialization that had commenced under the dictatorship. Unemployment reached a historic peak (19 percent in 1995), and the proportion of informal workers in the economy rose to 38 percent of the workforce in 2000. The least qualified low-income workers bore the brunt of this process, which culminated in a significant rise in the wage gap. In 1990, the richest were earning 18.4 percent more than the poor; a decade later, this percentage had risen to 24.8 percent (Delfini and Pichetti 2005).

Although it reduced state protection for salaried workers through measures such as the privatization of retirement pensions, the Menem administration did provide welfare to the poor and to others excluded from the job market as part of state policy (Franco 1996). In an attempt to remedy the soaring levels of poverty and unemployment, this government developed social assistance programs financed with funding from the Inter-American Development Bank and the World Bank.

These political and social processes have impacted the ways in which the poor sectors organize in Argentina. The deterioration of the formal job market made the poor dependent on informal and illegal work, welfare, and charity. In response to the noxious effects of neoliberalism, the Peronist party reconfigured its own organization, becoming what Javier Auyero has called a "problem-solving network" (Auyero 2001) that distributed funds and resources among the poor. Steven Levitsky (2003) writes eloquently of this process when he claims that during the years of neoliberalism, the logics of the Peronist party changed along with its support base, which shifted from unions (formal workers) to beneficiaries of the spoils system living in marginal areas.

At the end of 2001, a major economic, social, and political crisis mobilized the population against neoliberal policies, and starting in 2003, a new political cycle began in Argentina. During the successive presidencies of Nestor Kirchner and his wife Cristina Fernández de Kirchner, the state invested in manufacturing, expanded the domestic market, and implemented a set of novel welfare policies that aimed to improve the critical situation of the most relegated social sectors. As a result, poverty and unemployment dwindled while welfare and urban infrastructure rose (Kessler 2014). Like their peers in Bolivia (Evo Morales), Venezuela (Hugo Chavez), Brazil (Luiz "Lula" da Silva and Dilma Rousseff), Ecuador (Nestor Correa), and Uruguay (Jose Mujica), the Kirchners established "market inclusion" as a paradigm of well-being for the poor. This paradigm repurposed public funding for the country's most marginal population, allowing them not just to eat but also to participate in the consumer market. Such government policies marked a shift from what I refer to as a "contention policy"—aimed at merely keeping the poor above the poverty line—to what I call a "rehabilitation policy," where the purpose of giving the poor money is to integrate them into the market and reactivate the entire economy (Wilkis 2014). For the Kirchner administrations, the rise in spending among the low-income sectors was proof that their social and economic policies were working. The country's poorest households saw their average monthly income quadruple in real terms between 2004 and 2013. The rich, in contrast, only saw theirs rise 2.6 times. This trend can also be seen in terms of spending: the gap between average spending per capita between rich and poor fell from 7.3 times to 5 times (*Informe Encuesta Nacional* 2014).

Bearing in mind these macro-level social and institutional processes, the pieces of money that I intend to describe in this book reveal the juxtaposition of job market exclusion—and the resulting dependence on informal and illegal monetary circuits, welfare, and so on—and integration into the consumer market through state money and credit access. This narrative reconstructs the complex money and power dynamics that configure the world of the poor in Buenos Aires.

Villa Olimpia: A Money Puzzle

"Money grows on trees here in Villa Olimpia," Mary said to me one cold winter morning as we passed a house under construction. She was clearly referring to the new access to money and consumer products that she, her family, and her neighbors were all enjoying, owing largely to conditional government cash transfers and a vigorous expansion of the lending market to low-income borrowers.

Between January and December 2008, I visited Mary's house at least three times a week.[4] I gradually gained the trust of Mary and her children, and through them, my network of informants expanded and diversified. The daily dynamics of Mary's household were a microcosm that revealed transformations across Villa Olimpia, a neighborhood that both government officials and residents alike considered an exemplary case of the changes Argentina had experienced since 2003. The government had invested heavily to create new jobs and improve urban infrastructure and marginal homes. President Nestor Kirchner himself had visited the neighborhood in person a few years during his term. Governors and mayors also came. Many locals remembered these visits, and they were quick to pull out their pictures with elected officials whenever the topic arose. When I visited Villa Olimpia that first time, an urbanization program was already well under way. As in the urban improvement projects in the *favelas* of Rio de Janeiro (Brakarz 2002), new cement-block houses were being constructed, and almost all homes were connected to electricity, running water, and gas. The goal was to modify the typical configuration of the *villas miserias*, where precarious houses are often built from discarded materials. The population density is extremely high and when homes do have public utilities, it is usually thanks to an illegal connection to the network (Cravino 2007). As a result of the urbanization program, many Villa Olimpia residents believed that the social and urban stigma associated with living in the slums was a thing of the past.

In the history of Villa Olimpia, October 1999 marked the start of a new period. A group of locals got together to occupy some twenty hectares of neighboring land belonging to the company Gas del Estado. A series of different factors led to the occupation, including the accusation that neighborhood leaders had been embezzling funds; frustration over promises not met by different administrations; and the brisk growth of Villa Olimpia's population, which expanded from 1,000 to 1,600 families between 1992 and 2008. The enormous empty plot allowed locals to dream of their own homes. For several months, a group squatted on the property in an impromptu camp, assigning lots and organizing a co-operative. Everyone seemed to agree that Luis Salcedo was the leader of this process.

Salcedo had virtually no political experience, which was seen as a virtue in times when the seasoned political leaders of Villa Olimpia were widely viewed as corrupt. In a context in which Peronism had gradually become a problem-solving network in marginalized neighborhoods (Auyero 2001), veteran community leaders could no longer get state officials to provide resources for the neighborhood, causing locals to lose trust in them. Thanks to the leadership Salcedo displayed in occupying the Gas del Estado property, he had replaced them. Now the success of both the urbanization project and the new leader would depend on closer ties with elected officials and with Peronist party members, the main supporters of both the project and Salcedo.

When Salcedo heard that I was doing research on the neighborhood's success story, he asked me to take a walk with him. He wanted to show me a building that had been demolished to make way for a new home. After a few minutes, we reached a pile of debris, and Salcedo said: "People around here used to only dream of a house if their son grew up to be a soccer player or a boxer. Now anyone can dream of a home of their own."

"What happened?"

"Well, people here understand that we got involved in politics to make the neighborhood a better place. Maybe someone who's not from here wouldn't get it because they always had a home. We don't preach Peronist doctrine, just the project to build houses and pave streets. Now, if you want to come in here and you tell me you've got a better plan than I've got, well, OK, then, tell me see it is and I'm on board."

"And otherwise?"

"You get on board with us."

"A new project for change after fifty years" was the slogan members of Salcedo's network repeated time and again. It represented a shift in political rhetoric. This widespread perception was also present in a brief lesson that a neighbor gave me as he pointed out Salcedo's house: "If you want to know how all this works, look over there. That's where it all starts."

In a short time, the process of urbanization (and Salcedo's political rise) made Villa Olimpia into the perfect place to understand the role of money in the life of the poor. The state began to allocate funds to the neighborhood to improve infrastructure and build houses, but it also provided money for residents through new jobs, welfare benefits, and funding for the activities carried out by Salcedo's political network.

In showing that the monetization of personal life in the United States at the turn of the twentieth century neither rationalized nor impersonalized social ties, Zelizer postulated that money should not be considered as a variable independent of the process requiring explanation. In other words, money's mere presence is not indicative of its role in social life. If we view money as an isolated fact, we tend to see it homogeneously, as if it always produced the same effects regardless of context. However, if we consider that its meanings depend on a morally informed hierarchy, as I propose in this book, we must examine the connections between pieces of money and differences in the way it is used within a monetary order. Villa Olimpia forced me to adopt this principle in order to understand power relations through money.

How This Book Is Organized

In 2015, a conference was held in Paris to celebrate the twentieth anniversary of *The Social Meaning of Money*. Zelizer, the main speaker, shared the changes she would make to the book if she had a chance to rewrite it. Besides mentioning that a new version should explore e-payments, Zelizer reflected on the need to incorporate so-called real monies into her argument, that is, those that exist on the market, in commercial relations. "Why was that problematic?" she asked. "Because the term 'special monies' suggests that the areas I discuss are anomalies or exceptions to value-free market money. Although the book explicitly disputes that conclusion, still its argument has often been misunderstood as applying only to marginal phenomena and not to the allegedly colorless monies exchanged in commercial or professional market transactions" (Zelizer 2016).

This reflection twenty years after the release of *The Social Meaning of Money* reveals that for Zelizer, the tenet of the sociology of money is its moral ubiquity, even when considering the main trends of the capitalist economy. This book expands on this tenet by simultaneously analyzing heterogeneous money exchanges among the urban poor in Buenos Aires. In the pages to come, I analyze the pieces of money circulating on formal, informal, and illegal markets, through welfare and NGO assistance, and around political, religious, and family ties.

This book reveals that sociology is not interested in analyzing money inasmuch as it is interested in the social realities money helps to shape. Money is morally ubiquitous because it has a hand in social orders, moral hierarchies, and power relations. Each chapter of this book supplements the previous chapter, showing that no piece of money is more moral than the next: all revolve around the efforts to establish, appropriate, and accumulate moral capital.

In the first chapter, "Lent Money," I explore the expansion of the credit market to the poor working classes. The stories I share reveal how moral capital is critical to accessing this market and to the power relations it implies. In the second chapter, "Earned Money," I analyze the moral hierarchies that appear on the underground economy of Villa Olimpia. The third chapter, "Donated Money," recounts the moral struggles associated with being on welfare. For example, the money received in the new conditional cash transfer programs is associated with the power to determine who is deserving of such assistance. Power relations among political leaders and their followers are the topic of the fourth chapter, "Political Money," which focuses on the money that leaders pay their supporters. In the fifth chapter, "Sacrificed Money," I analyze the competition between political and religious leaders of Villa Olimpia, showing how these power struggles are rooted in the accumulation of moral capital associated with the pieces of money. Finally, in chapter 6, "Safeguarded Money," I analyze how family hierarchies and power are embedded in a monetary order and suggest that the various aspects of money help to produce both gender and generational hierarchies.

In the pages to come, money appears as a conceptual and methodological tool. This book offers a new focus for interpreting the multiple power relations that configure the world of the poor. Through it, I'll explore spheres of social life that are generally analyzed separately. Along this path, the moral dimension of money plays a critical role in forging economic, class, political, gender, and generational bonds. Instead of focusing on each of these spheres, this book aims to highlight the continuity between these, and by doing so, leaves little doubt as to the moral basis of money.

Lent Money

1

ONE SPRING AFTERNOON in 2008, Mary told me of a case where a family conflict was exacerbated by *lent* money. Her eldest daughter, Sandra, and her husband, Daniel, needed 3,500 pesos to move to a new house in Villa Olimpia. Sandra asked her uncle Jorge to lend them the money. The couple agreed with Sandra's uncle to wait until they had saved up the full amount of the debt before repaying him. However, the repayment occurred much more quickly than originally decided—and was distressing.

Two weeks after Sandra's uncle had lent them the money, the family got together to celebrate the birthday of one of Mary's other daughters. The dinner ended at around midnight. Mary was cleaning up the kitchen when she heard the voices start to rise out on the patio, where the others were playing cards.

The card game had been interrupted.

"Quit cheating."

"Who're you calling a cheater? You're the cheater and you always have been."

Jorge was the one shouting and slurring his words. It was clear he had had too much to drink. The more the others tried to calm him down, the more he insults he spewed. A few seconds later, he took the deck of cards and tossed it in Sandra's face.

Keeping in mind Jorge's generosity a few weeks earlier, Sandra's husband had not wanted to get involved. But he couldn't hold back when he saw his wife being mistreated.

"Come out onto the street and fight like a man, instead of going after a woman."

"What's your problem?" Jorge responded. "Everyone here knows you can't even pay your bills."

Daniel's expression changed; he turned on his heel and left. Sandra saw the look in his eye and knew he was heading home for his gun. She rushed after him, followed by her siblings. While they reached the couple's new home, Uncle Jorge came staggering behind them shouting, "I want my money. You're never going to pay me back, because you're a deadbeat."

Mary remembered that dramatic night all too well. The quarrel went on for hours. Jorge kept saying that they would never return the loan; he humiliated them outside their home, for all their relatives and neighbors to see and hear, before finally heading off to bed. The whole affair ended early the next morning, when several of Sandra's siblings and Daniel managed to come up with the full amount of the loan.

With the money in hand, they went to the uncle's house. They counted out the bills and handed them over. They hadn't spoken since.

Jorge had toyed with the uncertainty implicit in the return of any loan and inflicted humiliation by publicly expressing his doubt. "Everyone here knows you can't even pay your bills," he had announced in front of the whole family. Not returning the loan at that point would have been unbearable for Sandra's husband. He weighed two different options—settling the score violently or taking out another loan—and opted for the second.

Violence as an alternative response to being accused of financial unreliability reveals the emotional and economic weight of this public affront. In an economy of credit and debt based on interpersonal relations, the stigma of not repaying a debt is so strong that resorting to use of a weapon comes to seem a way to avoid potential economic and moral exclusion.

This is not a new argument. Different scholars in historiography (Fontaine 2008), sociology (Caplovitz 1967), and anthropology (Lomnitz 1975) have analyzed the moral dimension of loans and debt among the poor. However, the financialization of everyday life (Langley 2008) adds new questions to this hypothesis. One of the features of this process has been an expanded offering of consumer credit (Guseva 2008). In Argentina and in other parts of the world, the capitalist credit market now plays a key role in the economic lives of the poor (McFall 2014; Deville 2015; James 2015).

As a result of this process, there has been a return to one-sided narratives of credit and debt. In the past, classic works in anthropology and sociology have essentialized both formal capitalist loans and their alternatives, be they community-based (Geertz 1962) or informal loans (Caplovitz 1967). These narratives proposed a simplistic equation in which morality is treated as the flip side to capitalist credit.

There are two different yet complementary explanations for the recent return to these one-sided narratives. The first is the widespread use of new technologies for evaluating creditworthiness. Such technologies tend to evaluate one's capacity for repayment in terms of objective, measurable data, leaving moral or subjective elements out of the equation (Marron 2007; Carruthers and Ariovich 2010). As the Greek economist Costas Lapavitsas has noted, "The capitalist credit system is a set of institutional mechanisms focused on a formal mechanism of measuring trust. Since trust is objective and social, the moral force in capitalist credit is weak" (Lapavitsas 2007, 418). On the other hand, many defend "alternative financial" forms such as microlending (Maurer 2012), arguing that they add a new ethical dimension to the economy (Schuster 2015). My approach questions these narratives, since I do not consider morality as separate from capitalist credit or alternative finance.

The success of credit relationships depends on reducing uncertainty and anticipating the risks of not getting repaid (Knight 1921). Credit systems vary according to the way in which guarantees and credit scoring technologies are combined. Martha Poon (2009) has described the evolution of credit in the United States and the growing role of scoring technologies. In her work on French banks, Jeanne Lazarus (2011) analyzes how loan approvals combine moral assessments with objective indicators like job stability, place of residence, and so forth.

The notion of moral capital shows how uncertainty is reduced through a moral assessment of the borrowers. To contribute to current discussions about the moral dimension of credit and debt in everyday life (Peebles 2010;

Graeber 2011; Gregory 2012), I propose considering the concept of moral capital in this book as a kind of guarantee, together with other kinds of capital, such as economic or legal capital, analyzing how the different guarantees interact, and how moral capital influences the process. This perspective sheds light on the "classification situations" (Fourcade and Healy 2013) within credit systems that influence the chances of people and groups.

From this perspective, moral capital is produced and in turn produces power relations when it serves as at least a partial guarantee of *lent* money. The financialization of the economy shapes the economic life of the poor, creating chances for distinction and moral domination. The poor must ensure that their virtues are conspicuous in order to access credit. By examining how consumer credit began expanding to low-income sectors in Argentina in 2003, this chapter unveils the moral hierarchies rooted in the circulation of *lent* money.

Financing Dreams of Consumption

While Mary anxiously waited to buy a new fridge with her friend's credit card, her children were buying new clothes and tennis shoes with charge cards from local department stores. Some of her neighbors were making payments on personal loans from one of the many lending agencies that had been popping up near Villa Olimpia in the past few years. Many residents had bought furniture or home appliance on installments, with payback terms that took into account their variable incomes. Everyone in this low-income neighborhood was taking advantage of the new opportunities to make retail purchases and take out loans.

After the crisis in 2001 nearly brought banking activity to a standstill in Argentina, new trends transformed the field of credit.[1] First of all, financing for retail purchases increased between 2003 and 2012. In absolute terms, consumer loans in pesos rose from AR$4.54 million in January 2003 to AR$106.3 million in April 2012, an astronomical rise in nine years, even considering inflation. In January 2003, consumer loans in pesos represented just 15.5 percent of the lending market, while 40.5 percent corresponded to retail loans and 44 percent to mortgages. In April 2012, consumer loans had risen to 41.2 percent of all lending in pesos, while 40.8 percent corresponded to bank loans and 18 percent to property loans.[2] The credit market expanded as part of its diversification and segmentation. New loan strategies were unveiled, with a wide variety of bank loans and credit and charge cards;[3] loans from lending agencies; loans from major supermarkets and clothing and home appliance stores; and loans from mutual funds and credit unions. Each lending instrument had its own particular prerequisites. To qualify for a bank loan or credit card, applicants needed a higher income and more years of employment. Non-bank loans were easier to come by, but payback terms were shorter and interest rates were higher; when it came to plastic, the interest rate on charge cards—easier to obtain than a Visa or MasterCard—was 35 percent higher than that of credit cards (D'Onofrio 2008).

The diversification and segmentation of the credit market allowed new social sectors to access formal credit. While this benefited the middle class, who recovered the purchasing power they had lost during the 1990s and then again during the 2001 crisis, the lower classes have also seized on the expanded access to credit to become borrowers.

In December 2009, I organized a survey on lending practices in the retail shopping area known as CyC (short for Crovara and Cristianía, two intersecting avenues), a shopping area just four kilometers from the San Justo shopping mall, in La Matanza, a district in greater Buenos Aires west of the capital. Whereas the San Justo mall sold brand-name clothing and featured major home appliance stores like Frávega, Garbarino, and Casa Márquez, CyC has more in common with informal markets like La Salada, with knock-offs of big brand garments and tennis shoes.

The one hundred adults that comprised the sample included inhabitants of the nearby slums. The survey was designed to gauge ownership of household appliances and personal devices; it found that between 70 and 100 percent of those interviewed owned cell phones, music players, refrigerators, washing machines, and televisions or DVD players. In most cases, credit helped them finance these purchases. Survey takers stated that they had used loans to purchase their televisions (44.2 percent), DVD players (34.6 percent), washing machines (47.7 percent), refrigerators (66 percent), music players (46.7 percent), and cell phones (52.2 percent). These indicators shed light on the expansion of the credit market:

In a seminal paper, the anthropologist Clifford Geertz (1962) proposed that the informal lending networks in Asia and Africa played a key role in the transition from traditional economic systems to modern ones. In such networks, Geertz argued, people adopt the economic ethics necessary to socialize in modern institutions such as banks. Bourdieu et al. (1963) also offered a consequentialist argument on the evolution of lending practices in France after World War II. For these authors, this expansion of credit helped shift economic behaviors and ethics from pre-capitalism to capitalism. Finally, in another pioneering work, David Caplovitz (1967) analyzed how informal lending practices among the poor constituted deviations from the formal system of the retail market.

However, the data from the CyC survey contribute to a different interpretation of the way in which the credit market expanded among the lower classes in greater Buenos Aires. In addition to the rise in the money *lent* for consumer purchases, the social bonds and contexts of lending have become increasingly heterogeneous, as can be seen in the survey (Table 1). Those who took the survey reported many different lending options, such as bank loans and other types of formal credit (bank loans, credit cards, credit unions, installment plans at stores); informal financing (lending agencies, layaway); family financing (loans from relatives); neighborhood financing (buying on credit at neighborhood shops) or both (informal lending networks).

The fact that social lending bonds are so heterogeneous contradicts the argument that reciprocity networks are the most common source of financing. For the inhabitants of slums, financing can be based on interpersonal bonds (family assistance, buying on credit from local stores), but it can also be obtained on the expanding credit market, through credit cards and loans from lending agencies. These loans have fewer formal requirements than banks, although their interest rates are higher. Among the slum inhabitants who took the survey, 21.4 percent had requested loans of this kind (a percentage 1.4 percent higher than the total for the category of informal lending).

When considering all sources of financing, it becomes clear that microcredit from the government and NGOs is scarce. According to the survey

Table 1. Use of credit in greater Buenos Aires (2009)

	Total	By the inhabitants of informal settlements
Bank	16.5%	18.5%
Lenders	7.5%	3.6%
Credit/charge cards	38.8%	35.7%
Family loans	28.8%	32.1%
Buying on credit at local neighborhood stores	25%	17.9%
Loans from lending agencies	20%	21.4%
Payment by installments (without a credit/ charge card)	16.3%	17.9%
Layaway	15%	17.9%
Microfinancing programs	1.3%	0%

Source: Survey by author.

percentages, credit has a major presence in the life of the poor, much more than public loans or NGO programs.[4]

Unlike the consequentialist argument (Geertz; Bourdieu et al.) or the deviational argument (Caplovitz), the loan practices of those who responded to the survey combined both informal and formal credit. Their practices do not fit with a model that associates informal lending with backwardness and tradition, while tying formal lending to development and progress. The survey responses also deviate from the interpretation associated with normal systems (formal lending) as against deviant systems (loans to the poor).

The frequent use of credit cards and loans among the urban poor shows that credit has become a real possibility for nearly everyone: through the expansion of personal loans, financial institutions have absorbed those previously excluded from the banking system. However, this incorporation into the system has imposed particularly burdensome conditions on the poor.

Families in Debt

For Mauricio Lazzarato (2011) and David Graeber (2011), contemporary financial domination is represented by the figure of the *indebted man*. These authors suggest a new subjectivity that combines calculations based on the knowledge of credit technologies and one's own moral responsibility in relation to the risk of accumulating debt. In this chapter and the next, I want to shift the focus from individual subjectivity to the collective dynamics of credit and debt. In this section, my main goal is to show that families—not just individuals—go into debt. The concept of moral capital helps unveil the dynamics of self-discipline within families in relation to accumulating debt. For this reason, I am interested in the thoughts and feelings that contribute to a belief in the virtue of paying debts in a context of greater pressure to take out loans even among low-income families. My interpretation suggests that families turn this pressure into a vehicle for moral distinction.

To develop this idea, I tracked eight households in an informal settlement in greater Buenos Aires, asking families to keep track of their income and expenditures for one month using a spreadsheet. I then conducted interviews with the families to discuss their finances at the end of the month. We'll look at the percentage of debt in each household and later analyze the strategies each family uses to juggle their financial priorities (for comparison, in 2011, with a fluctuating exchange rate, from 3.4 to 3.8 Argentinian pesos were equivalent to a U.S. dollar):

- The Ortega family reported a total income of AR$3,650, AR$1,800 of which was the salary of the household head, and the rest welfare (two child allowances and a stipend for participating in a government work program). That month, the family paid around AR$1,500 pesos in charge card and credit card installments. Debt thus represented 41 percent of the family's monthly income.

- The Romero family reported a total income of AR$4,000 pesos. Of this total, AR$1,770 went to paying off debts. This was the breakdown: AR$1,100 pesos for a payment on an AR$8,000 credit card debt incurred to purchase materials for home renovations; AR$350 for an installment on tennis shoes purchased at a sports equipment store; and AR$330 for an installment on sheets and armchairs purchased from a vendor who regularly visits the neighborhood. Debt payment thus represented 44.2 percent of the family's income that month.

- The total income of the Torres family was approximately AR$1,400 pesos that month. At the time of the interview, the family was paying monthly installments of AR$370 on a washing machine purchase and AR$200 on food purchases made with a supermarket charge card. The family had two cards: a credit card and a charge card. To make monthly payment on their debts, they were spending 40 percent of their monthly income.

- The Portillo family reported an income of AR$2,900 pesos: AR$1,400 from welfare and AR$1,500 from the job of the main breadwinner. They spent AR$600 pesos to pay off debt that month, including AR$400 on an installment payment for mattresses purchased from a vendor who sold to people on welfare; AR$120 for a monthly payment on a pair of tennis shoes purchased with a charge card lent to them by a close relative; and AR$80 for a payment on a set of sheets they purchased from a vendor who visits the neighborhood. Debt payment thus consumed 20 percent of their monthly income.

- The Juárez family had AR$2,500 in monthly income: AR$1,200 in welfare; AR$360 from one family member's job cleaning houses; AR$700 in social security; and AR$240 from the child allowance program. They paid installments on a television that a friend of the family had purchased for them on credit at a shop. They did not have their own credit or charge cards. Thirty percent of their monthly income was earmarked for debt payments.

- The Míguez family had a monthly income of AR$4,000, including AR$980 from the child allowance program; AR$1,200 in welfare; and AR$2,000, the monthly salary earned by the main breadwinner, who worked as a painter. During the month of the study, they had faced approximately AR$8,000 in debt, including a monthly installment of AR$1,000 for a refrigerator purchased the previous month at a home appliance store. They were supposed to be making weekly payments, but since they couldn't manage it, the debt continued to grow. They decided to return the refrigerator. They usually paid AR$300 per month in installments to a local vendor from the neighborhood who sold clothing from the La Salada market. Since they would no longer have monthly installments on the fridge to pay, they were now considering the possibility of buying a washing machine and a television at a home appliance store on credit.

- The income of the Herreras was around AR$3,000 pesos. This included AR$2,200, which is what the husband earned, and AR$800, which is what the wife made working as a seamstress. They did not have their own credit card, but they had used a relative's credit and charge cards to make some purchases. They were paying monthly installments of AR$1,400 on a computer purchased at a home appliance store. The cost of the installments had risen due to interest owed on late payments (during the month of the study, they made two monthly installments to catch up). Payments on their debts took up 46 percent of their monthly earnings.

- The Moreno family reported an income of approximately AR$2,100, including AR$1,100 from a temporary job held by the head of the household; AR$300 from a disability pension; and AR$880 from the child allowance program (AR$220 per child). They were paying between AR$700 and AR$900 on payments for items purchased on a relative's charge card, clothing they bought from a woman who sold in the neighborhood; and a debt with the local grocer. The payment of their debts represented between 30 percent and 40 percent of their monthly income and varied according to the constant fluctuations of the amount owed to the grocer.

These household budgets provide an objective view of the pluralist systems of *lent* money at work in household economies. The relationship between incomes and expenditures indicates the dependence on debt that stems from this plurality.

The credit story of the Pérez family illustrates this point. It all began when the main breadwinner, who worked at a butcher's, became formally employed. In the past, every time the family had needed to finance a purchase, the head of the household would ask his boss to be his guarantor at local shops so that the family could purchase goods in installments. The man also had a charge card from a sporting goods store, which he had obtained by merely presenting his ID. Once his job situation was formalized, however, he was able to access different charge cards.

His wife, who had become a beneficiary of a welfare program, was now also able to get her own charge card. At the time of the interview, the couple had three cards. They viewed the plastic as an expansion of their ability to accumulate goods, even though all it contributed to the household budget was debt. Credit offered the couple an alternative when there was no cash, a way to compensate for not having any money set aside for a rainy day: "We don't have savings but we do have debt," as Maria Pérez would say.

For this reason, the possibility of consuming more by accumulating debt was viewed as both an opportunity and a threat. "You can live off the *chapitas* [cards] but you can't breathe," explained Maria. "You never get out of debt. But it's the only way to live well, to have everything you need. I mean, how else would we celebrate the holidays? I don't have a dime and I have to feed the kids. So how do I get by? The card. I go out and buy food or whatever else I need." The interpretation that debt is "the only way to live well" can be seen objectively in the budget of the Pérez family. When the totals were tallied, debt represented 41 percent of their income.

The general expansion of credit alters the framing of calculations (Callon 1998). Debt is managed and incorporated as part of household budgets. It is assumed as a constant, and calculations take into account the higher prices that accompany the use of credit. Since these households are deeply in debt, families juggle their obligations to keep their budgets from becoming unsustainable. In the case of the Pérez family, this was achieved by choosing the maximum number of installments, thus paying higher prices in order to then take out other loans.

"I pay my bills and then I see how much money I've got left over. That's how I get by," was a phrase that echoed throughout the interviews. It was indicative of how important loan and credit payments were to the household economies of the poor. People make arguments, talk, do the numbers, and then make purchases in a process where financial stability is often disregarded. "We are never satisfied with what we have," one informant told me. As soon as we've bought something, we already want something else. We are always going to be *encuentado* [drowning in bills]. Without the bills, you've got nothing. We can't pay cash." Being *encuentado* means assuming the predominant position of debt in the family's economy. Relief only comes when a financial balance is achieved. "I've got no worries because I paid my bills," as one interviewee put it.

Debt imposes its own rhythm on the circulation of money within the family. It involves all family members, either directly or indirectly. Just as consumption cannot be considered an individual act but is often organized as part of family obligations (Miller 1998), the debt burden is socialized as well.

"Credit cards are the only way for us to live well." The people surveyed shared this conclusion, along with the virtue of maintaining good credit standing in order to be able to make retail purchases. Credit was a prerequisite for financing purchases and thus accessing the good life. From this perspective, certain family members are more responsible than others for preserving moral capital. The circulation of *lent* money carries an ethos of responsibility. Families think about credit and are aware of it every single day; debts are their vehicle for consumption. People who refuse credit are turning their backs on a better life. Once people are immersed in this economic and moral dynamic, they begin to emphasize the virtue of paying back what they owe. The financialized economic struggle creates a moral value for this (self-)recognition.

The Violence of Credit

As we saw in the previous section, families jealously protect their moral capital in order to gain access to the newly expanded consumer credit market. At the same time, they impose self-discipline on family members and socialize credit access and debt payment. In the stories I share in this section, I shift the focus from households to the stores and banks where moral capital alone serves as a guarantee for the money they lend to the urban poor. As will be shown, this strategy helps stores and banks competing against one another for low-income clients, who in turn exercise self-discipline in their finances in order to qualify for store and bank loans. Moral capital reveals how this dynamic between the supply and demand for credit forms the basis for power relations and moral hierarchies to access lent money. The Crovara and Cristianía retail area, just a few miles away from Villa Olimpia, serves to illustrate these ideas.

I visited Crovara and Cristianía for the first time in 2006. Analysts had focused on this intersection as the epicenter of the attacks on supermarkets and retail centers that had taken place during the hyperinflation of 1989, and later, during the explosion of the economic and social crisis in December 2001. In a context of profound economic recession, there were violent lootings of grocery stores, home appliance stores, and even clothing shops in poor neighborhoods around the country.[5] Similar lootings have also occurred at critical moments in cities in Brazil, Venezuela, and South Africa over the past three decades.

I wrote these notes during fieldwork with a colleague in 2007:

> We try to move along Crovara Avenue to drop off Tato and Walter, two members of the recycling co-op who live in the settlements near the avenue. The idea is to then continue on the road back to the city of Buenos Aires, but a group of one or two hundred people is blocking Crovara Avenue. They are milling around in front of a few shops. Expectation fills the air, as if something important is about to occur. Rumors that stores could be looted have been circulating all day. A policeman turns on his siren and the uniformed men keep a close eye on the protestors.
>
> "We'll get out here," said Walter.
>
> "Yeah," agrees Tato. "We want to be here for these people."
>
> "No, stay with us," we insisted. "We'll find another way to get you home."
>
> However, the danger that we sense clearly does not affect these two men the same way. Tato winks his eye at us and says, "Don't worry, we'll be fine. There's nothing to worry about."
>
> When they get out of the car, we realize that Tato and Walter probably want in on the action.

A few days later, we found out that they had stayed on the corner until midnight waiting for the looting to begin.

A trust had been broken because of past lootings. After that experience, how could local merchants sell on credit? What dimension of the financialization of the economy of the poor does this history evoke?

To answer this question, it is useful to consider the way in which the offer of credit expanded in a shopping area like CyC. While the credit selection was becoming more diversified in San Justo, it remained reduced and stagnant in CyC. In San Justo, people could opt for credit cards and loans through loan agencies; in CyC, few businesses worked with agencies and none accepted credit cards. The personal loan agencies were located in San Justo near the stores, but there were none around CyC.

This uneven access to credit was expressed in the overall sales percentage. According to San Justo retailers, between 30 and 40 percent of sales involved some form of credit, while at CyC, lending instruments of any kind were practically nonexistent. This was confirmed in the data gathered during a survey conducted at CyC. Table 2 shows that credit is used more frequently at major retail chains; its use drops significantly at other types of stores, like those in the CyC shopping area.

The offer of credit at stores in the two areas shows that the financialization of purchases is by no means the same everywhere. The stores that adapted to the rules of this new economic scenario (those in San Justo) sold more. The CyC, in contrast, was the place for stores that did not have enough capital to offer formal credit instruments.

The survey of the CyC retailers provides revealing information. The retailers reported that they did not offer cards or credits through lending agencies because this would reduce their earnings. The principal reasons they listed were the following: the monthly maintenance fee on bank accounts, credit card commissions, and the taxes that they would have to pay if sales were declared to the tax authority. In other words, the CyC retailers did not have the economic capital to compete with retail chains and other stores with a diversified, extensive selection of credit options for consumers.

In San Justo, the poor had access to several types of credit. While the large retail chains in San Justo catered to a group that could be described as "lower class with a payroll stub," other retailers in this area offered credit instruments with no type of formal requirements. These instruments, however, were not available at the CyC stores.

The (Dis)Credit of the Lootings

Towards the end of 2009, the Argentine newspaper *Página/12* ran a story entitled "Holiday Rumors." "In La Matanza, rumors have been spreading

TABLE 2. Retail credit available to the inhabitants of informal settlements in greater Buenos Aires (2009)

	Percentage of purchases made on credit	CyC stores that offer some form of credit	Major stores in San Justo that offer some form of credit
Televisions	44.2%	18%	81.1%
DVD players	34.6%	47.6%	47.6%
Washing machines	47.7%	43.3%	53.3%
Refrigerators	66%	28.6%	65.7%
Computers	48.3%	28.6%	66.7%
Cell phones	52.2%	22.2%	72.2%

Source: Survey by author.

over the past few weeks . . ." began the article, which reported that before Christmas, there would be lootings similar to those that had occurred at the peak of the economic crisis in December 2001. "The people who live here say they hear the same rumor every year," continues the article, which describes Cristianía Avenue as the dividing line between two neighborhoods.

The *Página/12* article mentions the stigma associated with the neighborhood's residents since the economic and institutional crisis eight years earlier. One woman interviewed, Rosa Carrizo, acknowledged that she had heard rumors about the looting from her neighbors and from the mothers of her son's classmates at school. "Get ready," they had told her. Another woman interviewed by the press, an older woman named Marita, had some tips for avoiding the crisis. "You know what I would do? What the right thing to do would be? Any merchant who's afraid of being looted should get a bag of stuff ready to give to the needy. They wouldn't be any the poorer."

The prejudice suffered by the residents of the neighborhoods near CyC reasserts the crime and laziness often associated with the poor. When asked to describe their customers, one CyC merchant said, "They're all lazy. They come by in the morning, in the afternoon . . . No one works. They live off welfare." These two beliefs forged a retail relationship based on discriminating against the customer, a discrimination exacerbated by the looting of local stores.

The memory of the violence among local merchants could be seen in their everyday treatment of customers. "The store windows have been covered with bars since the lootings in 2001," reported the newspaper. The wife of an owner of a local clothing store was a good example of how this relationship played out, according to one resident: "After the looting, there was a lot of resentment. Everyone was thinking, 'Oh, sure, now you come to shop here . . .' The merchants on this block defended their businesses and once the danger had passed, they had to open their doors to those who had looted their stores. They had to just accept it. So it wasn't only about cutting their losses, it was about dealing with the anger," she explained, adding, "Take the owner of this place next door—she never waits on anybody. The store can be packed with customers, the employees running around trying to do everything and she won't even take the money when a customer wants to pay. She doesn't want to wait on them. She feels betrayed. We know who was responsible. Here we all know each other."

The merchants felt "anger," "resentment," and "indignation" towards their customers, but they also depended on them. In the words of one shop owner, "We have to swallow our pride." "Why don't they close up shop here and open up someplace else?" I asked her and others. For many of these people, their economic capital kept them from abandoning this retail space. The rentals on shops in downtown San Justo could cost triple those of CyC. The question, then, was how to provide credit instruments to customers who provoked "indignation," "resentment," and "anger" while providing financing to make their stores more competitive.

Given this panorama, it is no coincidence that lending instruments are so rare in CyC. However, certain credit practices enabled merchants both to boost their sales through financing and minimize the risk of providing credit to "untrustworthy" customers.

Layaway was a new practice that adapted to this retail configuration. For relatively inexpensive products such as clothing or shoes, the down payment and pickup could take place in a single month; for more expensive products such as furniture and home appliances, customers could take up to four months to finish paying for the item. Paying the original sale price with no markup depended on the store and on the item: for relatively inexpensive products, the price remained the same, since the purchase was completed within a month or so. For more expensive items, the price could be adjusted for inflation, depending on how long it took the customer to pay for them.

The customers' lack of cash and the fact that they had no access to formal financing cast them in a bad light for vendors; in addition, customers were seen as having no morals. The result was a payment instrument (layaway) in which the trustworthy subject was not the borrower but the lender. Unlike other credit practices based on the credibility of the borrower, who must provide evidence of being creditworthy, layaway works in exactly the opposite way. Through this payment instrument, customers can never become trustworthy subjects. Layaway strips agents of the moral capital they would need to enter into a credit relationship. Instead, retailers are entrusted with all the aspects of the marketplace transaction: keeping a record of payments made, maintaining or increasing the price, and assuring that the product will be in stock when it is paid off.

"People leave here with a slip of paper—it's not a receipt," explained an employee at one of the shops. "Anyone who's finished high school knows not to leave without a receipt, but for them, it's the only way to buy."

The buyers took two risks. If the price of the product went up, they would pay more for it. And when they were ready to pay off the product, it might or might not be in stock. Buying on layaway was a race against time to avoid these risks as well as the high cost of financing. For retailers, a moral rupture had been branded into their memory when they had seen their usual customers join in the lootings. "I saw guys looting who come in here and spend two hundred pesos on pants," said one retailer. "They weren't looting because they were hungry—they were taking everything they could," said another vendor, in reference to those who made off with alcoholic beverages and home appliances. Layaway was thus the economic cost of the negative moral consequences of the lootings.

Trust and Credit

On the opposite side of this devaluation of the moral capital of those who live in the neighborhoods surrounding CyC, there was another credit relationship that sustained a collective moral capital over the years. This story links the inhabitants of Villa Olimpia with a home appliance retailer in San Justo.

During my fieldwork in the neighborhood, the name of one store came up over and over again: Obrihogar, which had been in San Justo since the 1960s. Even in casual conversations, the interviewees mentioned a home appliance purchased on some type of credit at Obrihogar. Their relations with this store went back years, when one of the owners visited Villa Olimpia to offer the store's products in installments. This practice laid the foundation for the residents to purchase at Obrihogar using informal financing. "We go where [the major home appliance chain] Frávega doesn't go," said Omar when asked what distinguished his shop from its competitors. He was not speaking of physical distance—Obrihogar is located on the same block as a Frávega branch—but of symbolic distance.

Frávega will not offer credit to anyone who cannot provide a payroll stub. In contrast, Obrihogar offers its customers a triple incentive: a less hostile retail space ("Just imagine—people come in here in their work clothes. How do you think they feel at Frávega when the employees come over to them in uniform?"); credit without proof of earnings; and sympathy when customers fall behind on installments.

Being from the neighborhood is an incredibly important resource when it comes to believing that the borrower will pay back what he/she owes and is trustworthy. "Villa Olimpia residents pay what they owe," said the owner of Obrihogar. "But those who live in Villega de Santos Vega (another slum in La Matanza) are not as likely to pay."

Sustaining this moral judgment means thinking about a social network that allows Villa Olimpia inhabitants to purchase on account at Obrihogar. This network imposes a responsibility on neighborhood residents, since the discredit of not paying back a debt could jeopardize Villa Olimpia's status as a community that pays its debts. Given that existing customers introduce new customers and serve as guarantors, the social network acts as a filter, maintaining the credit rating that the neighborhood has earned at the store. Not all residents access this guaranteed introduction—only those who meet the prerequisites.

Maintaining initial moral judgments within the framework of stable social networks makes creditors better at anticipating what borrowers will do.

At the same time, borrowers are more likely to protect this moral capital, since it is the only guarantee they have to offer lenders. In this credit system, other types of guarantees are subordinate to moral capital. The absence of reliable information on income, job status, or credit history leads people to prioritize interpersonal trust in order to reduce uncertainty. Alya Guseva (2008) has analyzed a similar mechanism at work in the expansion of the credit card market in Russia.

This credit system can be interpreted by the way the store has worked to form bonds with the poor and offer them some type of financing. At the same time, credit is configured within individual customer relations, which reveal different possibilities for the use of credit instruments. Depending on the size, sales volume, and type of customer at each store, stores such as Obrihogar have been able to use moral capital to compete with major retail chains. The concept of moral capital thus entails different prerequisites for credit in large chains in comparison to small businesses, revealing how difficult it is for the most disregarded social sectors to access loans.

This unequal access to credit appears when reconstructing the social history of retail stores and the social basis for positive and negative opinions of borrowers among merchants. The study of the commercial configuration among Villa Olimpia residents and the Obrihogar store shows how the virtuous circle of moral capital can work.

The Heart of Capitalism

In this last section, I hope to show that this moral dimension of financial practices does not run counter to capitalist practices. The economization of morality (Çalışkan and Callon 2009) is a transaction that takes place not only along the margins but also in the heart of financing. This can be seen in the strategies used by banks to attract low-income customers.

"Hello. I would like to see about a loan," I told the employee at a credit agency in San Justo.

"Do you have a payroll stub?" asked the employee from behind a glass window.

"Yes."

"How long have you had your job?"

"About two years."

"Where do you live?"

"In Buenos Aires."

"Sorry . . . We only provide loans to people who live close by."

"Isn't Buenos Aires nearby? I came in here because I work near here."

"No, no. It's only for people who live nearby . . ."

"And why do you only provide loans to people who live nearby?"

"I don't know. That's the way the agency works. It's not up to me."

"OK then. Just to get some more information: how much money do you lend at a time?"

"Four hundred pesos the first time and six hundred the second."

"And how much are the monthly payments?"

"Two hundred and forty-five pesos . . ."

However, I could tell the conversation was over as soon as the employee realized that I did not meet the prerequisites for the loan. Her eyes shifted to her computer monitor and she hurried to answer my last questions. Though she did not become unfriendly, she clearly wanted me to leave as soon as possible.

At the personal loan agency I visited in San Justo, the loan request process and credit approval was highly impersonal, a simple yes or no. The exchange between agency reps and potential borrowers was limited to a list of the required guarantees (an identification card and payroll stub), a phone call to confirm the applicant's address, and a few brief questions about paying back the loan. What made this offer attractive was that the application was approved or denied so quickly. Anyone who did not have the documentation to prove who they were or how much they made was instantly informed that they did not qualify.

The distribution of space within the agency contributed to the process. The customer service windows were located all in a row and those waiting to speak with a rep stood in line right behind the person at the window. This meant that everyone could hear the conversations between the employees and the customers. This layout eliminated any privacy that would allow for more personalized treatment, as if to reiterate that this agency was only interested in a person's ability to prove where they lived and how much they made.

With this documentation, the loan amount is calculated in an economic transaction based exclusively on how much a person earns according to his/her payroll stub. The agency rep does not serve as an economic advisor or counselor but merely checks to ensure that the applicant meets all the prerequisites. These reps have no autonomy, as can be seen in the employee's response to me: "I don't know. That's the way the agency works. It's not up to me." This work method avoids personalized treatment altogether.

The process by which private institutions other than banks provide personal credit is highly indicative of how the poor have been incorporated into the financial system. Based on the interactions between the borrowers and the institutional representatives, objective and impersonal evaluation methods are used. Potential borrowers must present evidence of job stability and domicile (Lazarus 2011) and provide guarantees that they are moving towards a predictable future. The expansion of this personal credit market would seem to exclude moral capital from among these guarantees.

The development of technologies for evaluating borrowers shows a trend towards objective, quantifiable methods like scoring or rating systems (Marron 2007). This, however, does not capture the ubiquity of morality in lending systems. Fieldwork notes I took at another bank with lending strategies aimed specifically at low-income customers are particularly instructive in this regard.

"We also consider the way people live, no matter how poor they are. You can live in a slum or in a house built out of cardboard but still keep things neat. That says a lot about someone, about how responsible they are," Mario explains.

Mario is not a Catholic volunteer or a social worker who visits the slums. He is an employee at Elektra, a credit agency and home appliance sales company that is a subsidiary of Banco Azteca, which belongs to the powerful Mexican economic group Salinas. It is Mario's job to evaluate whether to give someone credit so they can purchase a home appliance. His assessment is not done from behind a glass window in an impersonal office: he visits the home of the applicants, where he is able to assess minute details of their personal life and values.

Banco Azteca was founded in 2002 in Mexico, where the bank has 1,500 branches and 15 million customers. Branches soon opened in other countries of Latin America, including Brazil, Peru, Guatemala, Honduras, and Panama. The bank has operated in Argentina since 2007 under the trade name Elektra. Unlike large banks with branches in downtown Buenos Aires, the first branch of this financial institution and home appliance store opened in the low-income neighborhood of Laferrere. Elektra now has another thirty branches. In order to adapt to a small economy, it offers loans that can be paid back in weekly installments. At the stores, instead of showing prices, signs show the number of installments with interest rates that range between 60 and 110 percent. The agencies also offer cash loans and money transfers.

In cases like Elektra or FIE Gran Poder—another company that offers financial products to low-income people in Bolivia and Argentina—offering credit to people excluded from the banking system means redefining the poor as consumers. This strategy was accompanied by a particular type of credit scoring. One of the features of credit approval is having trained personnel such as Mario visit the homes of the applicants to assess their environment. The principal aim of these visits is to establish a personal bond with the applicant, conduct a moral evaluation and get an idea of his or her private life.

> "It's important to gauge how friendly people are, because we have to be able to enter their house. This is one of the barriers we have to overcome: making people trust us enough to let us in. There are people who leave you standing in the living room and you have to use your arm to write on. Then there are others who invite you to sit down, offer you a glass of juice or water."
>
> Not everyone Mario sees has good manners. "That also lets you know how people really are—being polite, no matter how poor. You can sound out what these people are like. In general, the polite ones pay back their loans." The main purpose of Mario's visits is to establish a personal bond with the applicant, conduct a moral evaluation and get an idea of how they live.

Elektra combines different guarantees (economic, legal, and moral) and ranks them according to importance. It has constructed a market niche by selecting customers with few legal or economic guarantees but strong moral ones. Financing agencies like these publicize the fact that their lending is based on the guarantee I refer to here as moral capital; in other words, they make the recognition of moral virtues into standardized procedures. Moral capital is thus located at the core of capitalist finances—not on the fringes. According to C. K. Prahalad (2005), Elektra is the kind of company that sees a business opportunity in the people at the bottom of the pyramid. Prahalad argues that this is a profitable enterprise because of the poor's enormous and generally unexploited capacity for consumption. Based on success stories like that of Elektra, major companies should stop viewing the poor as underprivileged and instead treat them as a potential market (Elyachar 2012).

> Mario describes a typical customer as follows: "The men generally work in construction and the women as maids or seamstresses. They are part of the informal economy."
> "How much money does the company lend someone?"
> "Between five hundred and two thousand pesos if they don't have a way to verify their income. If they can verify their income, up to three thousand five hundred. Yesterday I saw a fellow who sells sausage sandwiches. He wants to clean up his cart, make it look nicer, and two thousand pesos is plenty for him. At the same time, that's the perfect amount for us to lend, knowing he will be able to pay us back. Most are cases like his."

An executive from FIE Gran Poder describes their credit assessment as follows: "The technology we apply here was tried and tested in Bolivia. We do interviews with friends and relatives to determine whether the person is trustworthy. We try to measure their willingness to pay and in this regard, the family plays a very important role. Being late on payments increases when there are family problems" (Sainz 2009).

While the dominant narrative of the expansion of the credit market tends to depict credit classifications as depersonalized and invisible, with a focus on economic and legal guarantees, here we discover exactly the opposite: a face-to-face, highly personalized interaction where moral virtues are assessed. In this credit relationship, other types of guarantees are subordinate to moral capital. Moral capital sheds light on the forces at work within the thoughts and feelings associated with credit.

> Now Mario describes his ideal client: "He doesn't have a payroll stub. He

does any old job and gets paid on a daily or weekly basis. He handles a bit of money, not much, but he isn't able to improve his living situation because he doesn't know how to save or get loans. The first time a customer told me, 'You're helping my dream come true,' I thought he was exaggerating." Pausing for a moment, Mario then added, "But over time, experience taught me the contrary: these people have a dream, something they're after. The customer I am looking for is someone who doesn't usually qualify for credit and we give him or her that possibility. At one training session, I was told that a customer makes sure to pay off a loan when it helps him make a dream come true: a dream like owning a television and a DVD player so he can watch movies."

Mario's words reveal the figure of the poor meritocrat positioned at the heart of capitalist finance. "That is why the lower classes are the ones who take credit so seriously." Mario, in fact, has no interest in a customer who makes ten thousand pesos per month but never makes a payment.

"We're looking for profit. I'm good with the guy who gathers cardboard, gets by and pays me a fifty peso weekly installment. The ones who come in with a payroll stub are the ones who fall behind; some of them say, 'I can't make the payment because I've got to throw my daughter's fifteenth birthday party.' There are customers with a high credit rating who suddenly disappear . . . Once I went to see a guy who was avoiding me and I drove my scooter right into his garage because I was so angry. I am talking about company workers, factory supervisors, people who earn a decent salary . . . They're the ones who fall behind."

The success of this credit relationship depends on the belief in the credit-scoring technology described by Mario. One of the conditions of this belief is the conviction that formal, economic guarantees alone do not provide a solid basis for approving a loan. Sometimes this type of loan assessment is based on forming a bond with applicants whose "dreams will come true" if they are approved.

Mario insists: "These are people who cannot access credit and our company gives it to them, so they work hard to pay us back. It's a pleasure to help them. And if they don't make a payment, it's because something's gone wrong. I have cried alongside my customers when a serious problem comes up and they can't make a payment." The relationship, according to Mario, went beyond the usual one between a loan agent and a borrower. "I can now call many of these people my friends because they help us and I help them. When you help out people like this, they are on your side for life. Because they are careful with a loan—it's their only chance to buy a cell phone or a television set or whatever. That is why the poorest people are our best customers."

Mario's account has a precise performative value. It establishes a certain morality required to participate in this credit system. This implies a preconception of both the moral value of the meritocratic poor and the technical and emotional capacities for discovering this value. Mario was trained to believe in both preconceptions that give shape to this credit system.

These credit relationships may provoke discomfort. Like other alternative financial forms such as microcredits, they extend credit to those who have none, thus democratizing money. On the other hand, without demanding a more ethical economy, they economize moral virtues. But do they use other means to achieve the goals of alternative financing? If the practices that have been defined as "alternative" can adopt the features of the dominant financial practices (Maurer 2012), the opposite can also occur: dominant practices can take on the features of alternative financing. These "poor people's banks" shake the very foundations of "alternative financing" and suggest that the relationship between economy and morality is not a formula but an enigma.

In this first chapter, an initial inquiry into the meanings of money in the life of the poor led me to discover the piece of money *lent*. Instead of fitting perfectly into a unified and stable reality, though, it itself is a puzzle, incomplete and open to exploration. For this reason, the chapters that follow delve deeper into the meanings of the piece of *lent* money as new pieces of the puzzle are unveiled.

In a work that deconstructed Max Weber's myth of the capitalist spirit, the historian Craig Muldrew (1998) analyzed the origins of capitalism in England to show the importance of a credit as a "cultural currency" based on trust and a household reputation. Muldrew's work is quite similar to anthropological studies that attempt to explain the social and moral profiling that occurs in contemporary financing (Zaloom 2012; Ortiz 2013). Both approaches deconstruct the one-sided narrative of the morality of credit and debt. My work has moved in the same direction, seeking to deessentialize the opposition between informal and community-based systems and so-called capitalist systems. Instead, I reveal their similarities, showing that both systems require individuals to accumulate moral capital as a way to access credit and pay off debts.

Here we have seen the moral ubiquity of money *lent* in both the formal and informal situations where money circulates. I have also revealed how moral capital becomes a guarantee that sustains the power relations at the core of these situations. As we have seen throughout this chapter, for those with scarce economic and cultural assets, struggling to have one's values acknowledged is part of daily financial management. Moral capital is a passport. However, like all forms of acknowledgment, it is rare, which means that in order to access the material benefits capitalism has to offer some are forced to accept disadvantageous terms, like those of layaway. The hypothesis that moral capital multiplies economic capital suggests that there are inequalities among borrowers as they compete for moral distinction.

This chapter has focused on one of the dynamics that shapes the economy of the poor: the recent expansion of the lending market. The next chapter analyzes the power relations through the moral dimension of money *earned* on informal and illegal markets.

Earned Money

2

IN JUNE 2011, I traveled to the southern edge of greater Buenos Aires with Sebastian Hacher, a young journalist who was researching the La Salada market for a book he would later publish, *Sangre Salada*. In 2011, *Forbes* magazine called La Salada the largest informal market in South America.[1] Our trip was part of a plan to write a piece about the market for a local magazine. Hacher, who had been visiting for a few years as part of fieldwork of his own, led me into the labyrinth of booths.

The market had grown by leaps and bounds—and attracted international attention—after the economic and social crisis of 2001. However, it had been founded a decade earlier, when members of the Bolivian community took over an abandoned riverside recreational area and began renting sales booths to vendors. At the time of our visit, the market was still growing. In fact, it has expanded to nearly twenty-six acres, with more and more people arriving to buy and sell. According to estimates, 150,000 people from large or small cities across Argentina and from neighboring countries visit the market on each of the two nights it opens per week. The nightly sales of the nearly 30,000 booths can reach AR$150 million (Girón 2011). However, these numbers are not particularly reliable, as few hard facts on La Salada are actually available (Hacher 2011).

The piece that Hacher and I wrote was entitled "The Invisible China." It began:

It's almost midnight on a Tuesday and it's practically a miracle that this woman who just arrived from the province of Tucumán has found Doña Pilar the lingerie saleswomen, considering the thousands of booths selling everything from socks by the dozen to winter coats at ninety pesos each.

Finding Pilar in the sprawling market is doubly difficult. Her booth is not in Urkupiña, Ocean, or Punta Mogotes, the three traditional fairs in La Salada, but in an area within the market that began on the shores of the Riachuelo before crossing the street and spilling onto the sidewalks of the neighborhood. This grey zone has been named La Ribera (the shore), for lack of a better name. La Ribera is the edge of an edge, an extreme of extreme informality, the site where the struggle to sell an item that may have come from a sweatshop in Villa Celina or from a high-tech factory in southern China produces desperate cries like the one that now rises above the racket: "Three pairs for ten pesos, what a deal!"

Pilar Quispe is standing at her booth. Her eyes move back and forth, taking it all in: the merchandise, the people going by, the girl who helps her at the booth. She still wears her hair the way the Bolivian women do, in two long braids, and is dressed in a chiffon skirt that falls below the knee. She is friendly to everyone who stops to see her wares. She talks to the customer from Tucumán and pushes a broom stick up above her until she is standing on tiptoe. She leans on the counter and smiles when the hook at the end of the broom handle catches the hanger of a red bra perched from the ceiling of the booth.

"Sorry to make it so hard on you, Doña Pilar," says the buyer, "but I'll make out like a bandit with that bra. Give me the biggest size you have."

Pilar chortles out of courtesy. In fact, when this woman from Tucumán arrives every fortnight to buy lingerie—which she later resells to transvestites back in her province—she repeats the same line and Pilar laughs again. The saleswoman knows that this woman came 1,300 kilometers in a bus with seats that barely recline just for the cheap prices. She knows that the woman will travel back to her province that night and try to sell her wares as quickly as possible to repeat the cycle in a week or two, returning to the roads and the buses, to Ingeniero Budge and La Salada, her final destination. For Pilar, knowing that the woman from Tucumán is in a similar situation sparks a sort of class solidarity: both spend many a night sleeping on buses and moving suitcases filled with clothes for other people.

My Paraguayan contact Mary also used this popular business model, buying merchandise at La Salada and selling it to Villa Olimpia residents on credit. This *earned* money made Mary part of an underground retail circuit that the Brazilian anthropologist Gustavo Lins Ribeiro calls "globalization from below" (Lins Ribeiro 2012). The markets of the poor constitute nodes of dense retail networks involving many products—mainly knockoffs—with China as the main center of production, though by no means the only one. Rosana Pinheiro Machado (2011) has sketched out a global chain connecting people of different ethnic backgrounds who sell and buy goods in China, Paraguay, and Brazil. Her conclusions can also be applied to the sprawling market on the south side of greater Buenos Aires (and to others that have popped up across Latin America, like Galeria Pagé in São Paulo, Brazil; Tepito in Mexico City; and Ciudad del Este, Paraguay). Imported goods are sold at La Salada alongside products manufactured at local informal sweatshops (Gago 2012).

Mary's involvement in La Salada was connected to this transnational dynamic and also to a transnational monetary hierarchy that is used to interpret the world of the poor. The European Union has called it "the largest counterfeit market in Latin America." The local media have echoed this assessment, referring to La Salada as "The biggest source of knockoffs in Latin America," "A mega-market of fake products," "The counterfeit seekers' mecca," and "The poor people's mall."

These descriptions of money *earned* in a questionable way bring to mind certain narratives within the social sciences in which dichotomies are used to describe the world of the poor. For example, the lifestyle of Mary and her family is similar to what Elijah Anderson (1999) has referred to as the "code of the street," a code associated with crime and a lack of respect for the law. This goes against the code of "decent" families with mainstream values like efforts towards getting ahead, valuing hard work, and so forth.

This dichotomous narrative of the world of the poor has been questioned by certain researchers. Loïc Wacquant (2002) has described how this is a moralizing vision of the life of the poor that distinguishes the virtues of the "good" poor from the defects of the "bad" poor. In his ethnography of the underground economy of the marginal neighborhoods of Chicago, Sudhir Alladi Venkatesh (2006) challenges these narratives from another perspective. Instead of positioning actors according to rigid moral values, Venkatesh describes how people make decisions on illegal economic activities according to shifting contexts and their needs at any given moment.

This book proposes to explore the world of the poor in a way that also questions dichotomous narratives. Instead of defining the poor as decent or indecent, moral or immoral, it points to the way in which certain moral hierarchies come to bear on the circulation of money in the lives of residents of the low-income sectors of society. A dichotomous narrative overlooks what people have in common with the social worlds they inhabit; here I hope to show continuity. Like the world of family, politics, and religion, the underground economy has its own rules for the accumulating of moral value, obligations, and virtues. People maneuver their way in these worlds, adapting to rules that allow them to accumulate moral capital.

Exploring how the underground economy operates as a moral space of earning income reveals the dynamics of questioning and legitimizing what has to be done to earn money. The concept of moral capital is a useful tool for understanding how this monetary phase operates or is eliminated in response to a moral assessment of people's actions. Villa Olimpia contributes rich and heterogeneous subjects in this regard: merchants with small businesses who live in the slum; women who sell whatever they can, such as Avon cosmetics or clothing purchased elsewhere; numbers racketeers; young people who sell stolen products or drugs in the neighborhood; warehouses that buy recyclable garbage; sellers who offer furniture on credit. The underground economy presents a dense weave, which I attempt to unravel here by examining *earned* money.

The Informal Retail Sector

Marga's two-story cement house is located on block 32 of Villa Olimpia. The doorway of her grocery store and the gated window through which she sells to her customers face onto an alley flanked by makeshift houses. At the time of my last visit, her block had yet to be urbanized. Behind the house was a roadway where the inhabitants of Villa Olimpia came and went from the neighborhood at rush hour. Her business had its back turned to these potential clients.

Marga was hoping to put in a new door and window in order to attract more customers and improve the lighting. The alley was lit, but her house was dark, and that scared her. At night, she could hear the young people outside the door to her grocery store; she assumed they were drinking beer and smoking *paco*,[2] a drug that had ravaged marginal neighborhoods over the past few years.

Marga sold a diverse range of products, including beverages, food, cigarettes, and cleaning supplies. The refrigerators, freezer, and cold-cut slicer showed how much she had invested in her shop. When the temperature began to rise in late spring, she said proudly, "All I need is the ice cream and I'm set: I've got it all." The month of December was the most important on Marga's calendar, as the earnings of the year were determined in that final month of the year. She looked forward to it with anxiety and excitement.

Inside, it was difficult to distinguish the home from the store, as the merchandise overflowed into the other rooms. When it was delivered, Marga would put it in a room where she kept the store refrigerators and her washing machine—or stack it on the kitchen table. Cartons of drinks were left outside the storeroom, next to the bathroom. When the cartons were emptied, it freed up some room for her home, at least until the next delivery.

This mixed retail/home functionality required a subjective layout, with washing machine, fridge, and TV sharing space. Marga had to adapt her attitudes, opinions, and economic ethics from the business to the more intimate realm of the household.

Such adaptation cannot be termed a strategy of survival, one of the go-to concepts in Latin American social sciences when analyzing economic opportunities in marginal areas.[3] Lourdes Suárez describes these opportunities with respect to greater Buenos Aires as follows:

> The way in which households in marginalized settlements orchestrate their occupational strategies in order to earn enough to survive also fosters social isolation among the urban poor. These are strategies that sink "workers" deeper into their neighborhoods, submerging them in the precarious "job" opportunities that the neighborhood can provide. . . . It turns them into or-

chestrators "skilled" at getting by but in no way provides them with any opportunity for escaping their marginal position. (Suárez 2006)

Marga does not fit the image of someone living on the fringes, nor do her practices in relation to money *earned* evoke survival strategies. This gap between the way the poor are depicted and their actual economic practices makes it necessary to explore the conditions for accumulating and earning money in marginalized contexts.

I would sit down to talk with Marga in a narrow hall that connects her home to the grocery store. On television, Venezuelan accents announced the afternoon soap opera. Marga had told me that she took a break at this hour, but her work never ceased: we were constantly interrupted by the bell ringing to announce a new customer. In a little ritual, Marga would ask me to hold on a moment and when she came back from the store, she would pick right up from where she had left off. When she spent the afternoons alone watching the soap opera, she would do the same thing.

Although work was slower at this hour, Marga had an ear out for the bell. The store's layout reminded her of her first grocery store. At the beginning of the 1970s when she came to Villa Olimpia from Paraguay in one of the most important migratory waves in the neighborhood's history, Marga worked as a maid while her first husband was employed as a construction worker. As a couple, the gendered division of their work was typical. "When I worked as a maid, I earned a good living," she recalled. The money they saved during those years allowed the couple to buy the lot where they would build first a room and, years later, a house.

At the beginning of the 1980s, she got a job at a beauty school. When her first daughter was born, her husband asked her to stay at home. She agreed, but with the scarce savings she had, she insisted on purchasing merchandise in order to stay financially active and sell from home. The small initial investment was accompanied by a great deal of time and effort.

The business grew because of Marga's extreme opening hours. She often stayed up all night on Fridays and Saturdays to keep selling beer and cigarettes. A group of fellow Paraguayans would regularly get together outside the store to play cards and drink. She kept pace with them, but instead of drinking or playing, she would clean the house. She wouldn't go to sleep until the last of them, staggering drunk by that hour, had left the table set up at the shop entrance. Her husband complained that Marga was spending too much time on the store, but she wouldn't listen. She kept up that rhythm for several years, earning enough to invest even more.

By handling this *earned* money and learning about business, Marga gained economic independence from her husband. He was able to tolerate her working as long as he was still the main breadwinner: he accepted her contribution to the household, but drew the line when her income exceeded his. Other studies on the economy of the poor have pointed out how difficult it is for women merchants to escape this model, because they suffer the pressure associated with gender discrimination when it comes to handling numbers, money, and earnings (see Absi 2007 on Bolivia). Marga broke the mold by establishing a career as a merchant. As a result, her marriage ended. Her husband found it too hard to deal with her business's growth.

The time she spent in her store had left her with the conviction that hard work was essential. During one of my visits in November 2008, Marga was awaiting a call to confirm a hospital appointment. She needed an operation. The call still hadn't come, and Marga became increasingly worried as time passed and the holiday season neared. She could not possibly close the store for the holidays—those long-awaited weeks when business boomed like at no other time of the year.

"As long as you're able, you have to keep on working. Nothing's free in this world," she explained. "I want to get that operation and get out of here, see if I can get some peace and quiet." She was referring to her house in Paraguay, where she spent the month of January. "That's why I work. Whenever my kids ask, 'Why do you work so much?' that's what I say. As long as I can work, I don't want to hire anyone else to work here."

"Why not?"

"I just wouldn't get used to it. Plus, why would I stop working? I'll get sick if I do nothing." She soon expressed some contradictory thoughts on the matter, however. "I'd like to close the store, you know? Because there's no time to rest. I get to rest now because it's not so hot outside, so no one buys any ice cream. When it's hot, they come for ice cream nonstop. And not just ice cream. You have to have everything. If all the other stores close on Sunday, that's more reason for you to stay open. Having a store is nice, but you have to be there. It's exhausting. Many people close down because they're too tired. You want to rest and you close on Saturday or Sunday, but that doesn't make sense, because those are the days when business is booming. Monday is the day I rest the most, because business is slow, but then it picks up again."

Marga's time thus revolved around the set of feelings and perspectives of *earned* money. For that reason, she became fraught with tension after entering the world of political exchanges, a world that also required hours. The scarce time she had available was the common thread of many of our dialogues, and yet Marga clearly wanted to find the time for her political work to support Luis Salcedo.

Salcedo's political career was closely linked to the urbanization of Villa Olimpia. The home improvements, roadwork, and neighborhood infrastructure all contributed to his position as a leader. A great part of the political activity of Salcedo and his group involved resolving the urbanization issues residents were facing.

Marga hoped that Salcedo would send some people to add a back entrance to her house. That way, she could sell to passers-by on the road to the rear of it, but Salcedo kept postponing doing so. When it came to explaining why she wasn't going to attend meetings or marches where she might be able to ask Salcedo directly, Marga argued that she couldn't leave the store. She just didn't have the time.

"I want to talk to Salcedo and get him to give me a little more land, because my daughter wants her own room, her own house; to see about constructing another story, or adding on to the patio. I paid for my lot a long time ago. That's why I went to talk to Diego at the co-op: to get him to measure my property. I've got all the paperwork . . . Mary told me to go over there at five o'clock. But first I have to talk to Luis Salcedo. And you need time for that! I'd have to close the store. My daughter wants her own room now."

Her daughter was expecting a baby in a few months.

"My house is big but there are no extra rooms. The store takes up a lot of room and she wants to move upstairs. I have the right to the construction materials, the right to build the room. But you have to keep on their tails, and I can't. I need time! How can I close the store? There are still things I need to sell. I can't just leave."

This last remark reveals the close connection between work ethics and attitudes to time (Weber 2001 [1904–5]; Bourdieu 1977). For Marga, hard work went hand in hand with not letting time go to waste in economic terms. To compete with other stores, Marga kept hers open as many hours as possible until the year ended. Only then could she think of recreation or distraction.

"You're a slave to your store," she would say time and again. She associated the money she *earned* with economic independence. Her intense dedication to this business gave her autonomy. She did not want to renounce money *earned,* so she stuck to this hardworking attitude that had brought her so many benefits in the past. Her work ethic had been solidified through hard labor, which she viewed as the way to stay independent. In Marga's view, the money she *earned* was a source of her moral capital. As it circulated, she was able to recognize her own virtues, form a positive image of herself, and proudly recount all that she had been able to achieve because of her work in the store. However, the circulation of money *earned* and the accumulation of moral capital are wrought with tension. The opinions of her neighbors bring other moral assessments to bear on the money *earned.*

Marga had signed up to join Luis Salcedo's political group during an affiliation campaign in which Mary was visiting different neighbors to get them involved. I had accompanied Mary on that visit, and when I got in touch with Marga to ask her for an interview, she reminded me of something particular that happened the day we met.

"I'm no merchant. That's why when they came to sign me up, I told Mary to put housewife, not merchant, on my card. A merchant is someone with money, and I've got none. People think I earn a lot because I have the store. Look at my daughter's room!" she exclaimed, pointing to the small room where her daughter lived with her boyfriend. "And I work all the time."

For Marga, the word "merchant" meant access to a certain quantity of money *earned.* She did not want to be recognized as such; on the contrary, she actively denied any sign of accumulating money. Didn't she work all day long? Wasn't her pregnant daughter sharing a tiny little room off the terrace with her boyfriend? Thus, in spite of the economic privileges that had come from investing time and space in her business, a lack of space and time provoked a subjective resistance to being defined as a merchant. For

Marga, these were more than enough reasons to put her on the same social level as her neighbors, customers, and relatives. After all, like them, Marga lived in a slum. Her refusal to be perceived as a merchant showed the contradictory way in which she related to money *earned*. She could easily express the feelings and perspectives associated with the independence of this piece of the money puzzle; in contrast, she made every attempt to shake loose of them when they could be used to judge her. She was very aware of her earnings and how they had shaped her, but a fear of being judged by other residents of the slum made her refuse to be associated with those earnings. After all, a store was a place where money was exchanged in plain sight.

Like the other aspects of money examined in this book, money *earned* is impossible to decipher without taking into account the negotiated and often contradictory moral meanings that people attribute to it. Marga's insistence clearly reveals the tensions in her relationship to the money *earned* and her position in relation to her neighbors. Her pride in her successful business was at odds with the need to hide any sign of wealth in order to be seen as no different from anyone else in the neighborhood.

Marga's ambivalence shows how the moral space of money *earned* is framed by structures of legitimation and dissent. For her, being a merchant involved dealing with these tensions.

Money *Earned,* Money *Lent*

Marga was able to lend money to a neighbor who needed to travel to Paraguay to see a dying relative. At times, she provided work for relatives or neighbors. And most often, she resorted to *fiado* (credit) for certain customers. The money Marga *lent* to people in a pinch was one of her obligations. Regardless of whether the quantity was small or large, and whether the payback time was days or months, it was hard to fit in this *lent* money with the money she expected to *earn*. In the neighborhood, having a position associated with money *earned* required her to lend money to avoid being judged. However, this was difficult to negotiate.

When we discussed *fiado*, the tension associated with the topic became evident. She discussed the *clavos* ("nails," people who never paid back what they owed), summoning up old debts. Marga had the notebooks in which she kept track of the loans; these were her receipts. Once I offered to help her organize them. She responded flatly, "I don't need to organize them—I need to get paid."

These notebooks were evidence of how the *clavos* had let Marga down. "I helped them out and they don't appreciate it. When my children ask me how we managed to eat when we were hungry and I say, 'By working,' they say, 'How do you explain the *fiado* they didn't pay back?' I'm done with the *clavos*. Now I only give out a hundred or a hundred and fifty pesos per month." Marge looks down at the list with resignation; her own nephew was on the list, along with the amount of his unpaid bill. She murmured, "It's hard to ask people supporting a family to pay you back."

Although *fiado* may not be as common a practice between merchants and locals as it used to be,[4] it remains a way to close a transaction. Marga and owners of similar stores were regularly forced to deal in these terms. They could not elude *fiado* if they wanted to maintain their ranking in the neighborhood and have their business succeed. As Marga once told me, "Some customers think it's an obligation [*fiado*], but I make it clear that it's a favor."

Marga's contradictory feelings in relation to money *earned* are easier to comprehend if we see them as a tension between two sources of moral capital. On the one hand, money allowed Marga to recognize her own virtues and be proud of her achievements. Her neighbors, on the other hand, used different criteria to evaluate her success. For them, the money Marga *earned* meant that she could always give them a hand, providing them with money *lent*. The other source of moral capital—the other measure of her virtue—was the one that depended on whether or not she complied with these requests.

If Marga embodied the structured and intense ethics of retail, preoccupied with the capital investments she needed to offer new merchandise and maintain her equipment (refrigerators, freezers, and cold-cut slicers), Mary was on the opposite end of the spectrum. Her main activity was selling food on weekends at the local soccer field, where the entire neighborhood came together to watch matches. Her sons provided the meat that she used to make the empanadas and hamburgers she sold from the meat-packing factory where they worked, and the only equipment she needed was a grill, which she carried from her house to the soccer field. Moreover, this work took second place to her political activities in Salcedo's network.

While they were on opposite ends of the spectrum in terms of capital investment, there was another less perceptible but significant difference between the two women. Both were excessively exposed to the moral judgments of neighbors, customers, and relatives. Mary's business brought few demands in this regard. Marga, in contrast, was constantly subjected to judgments and biases. The fact that she was identified as a store owner put her in the moral sphere of earnings, from which Mary was practically excluded.

The two women's positions in the moral sphere of earnings reveal the objective pressures each of them faces. The uneven exposure to the biases of customers and neighbors translated into the pressure both faced when it came to offering credit transactions. Though this was not relevant in the case of Mary, for Marga, money *lent* was part of negotiating her status with respect to customers and neighbors. This argument reveals why Marga was resistant to being identified as a merchant, a role that entailed certain obligations in the moral sphere of earnings. By seeking to avoid classification as a merchant, she was trying, albeit unsuccessfully, to set herself free from these obligations.

This comparison between Marga and Mary allows us to see that people negotiate their moral status through the hierarchies established by different pieces of money. From the perspective of her retail activity, Mary was not subject to biases or challenges within the moral space of earnings; in contrast, in her activity within Luis Salcedo's political network, she was part of a system that regulated the accumulation of moral capital. Chapter 4 explores the notion of *political* money further; for now it suffices to say that as this money circulates, political loyalty to a leader is put to the test. Mary was immersed in this moral and monetary dynamic, and Salcedo acknowledged the work she was doing to ensure that the residents gave their support to him as the political leader. Mary's moral capital in politics depended on her meeting her obligations to Salcedo in this regard.

It's wasn't that Mary was more moral in her political activity and less so in her retail activity, but in the two activities she was judged by different monetary hierarchies. The same can be said of Marga. She was exposed to accumulating moral capital in the retail realm, not in the political one. This meant she was judged for the money she *earned* and excluded from the obligations of *political* money.

The Numbers Racket

Marcela and Cosme came to Villa Olimpia in 1972. Cosme, a plasterer by profession, had begun working in construction at a young age. Marcela was raising their children. For the locals, they were known as the *quinieleros*. Their house was easy to recognize: it was on the neighborhood's busiest street, and they hung signs on gated windows with the names of the lotteries people could play and the day's winning numbers. As a sign of her savoir faire in the numbers game, Marcela emphasized the importance of keeping the latest numbers posted. This was a way of showing how active they were in the business.

In the mid-1990s, jobs with the fewest qualifications—such as those in construction—suffered the most when unemployment began to rise. Cosme came up with an alternative: he would stop playing the numbers game and become a bookie instead. "I switched to the other side of the counter," he explained. Looking back, it was not a difficult transition. He just had to find a boss, who took a commission on the bets he took and in turn offered him protection from the police.

Until it was legalized in Argentina at the beginning of the twentieth century, the numbers game was illegal but tolerated. A century later, the lottery was still legal, but there was still a thriving market for illegal betting, mainly because the illegal betting centers were closer to people's homes and more convenient. Frequently mentioned in popular music and in Argentine literature, the *quinielero* is a regular among characters from the lower classes. Although there are no hard statistics, some estimate that this illegal market represents around a billion pesos a year (Figueiro 2012).

Marcela and Cosme felt confident and supported by their boss. He "took care of them," as they put it. In ten years, they had not had a single problem, no police harassment. They were confident that if a raid was planned, the boss would let them know well in advance. The boss would pay someone to pretend to be a numbers racketeer; the police would keep that person in jail overnight, but he would then get off for lack of evidence and witnesses. Agreements of this kind are not exceptional. Matías Dewey (2012) has shown how this protection—that is, receiving insider information on planned police raids—is one of the most coveted services the police provide and allows several illegal markets to thrive on the outskirts of Buenos Aires.

Cosme and Marcela were not the only *quinieleros* in Villa Olimpia. About fifteen people worked as numbers racketeers, that is, one per hundred inhabitants, a rate that indicated the importance of the numbers game in the life of the neighborhood. Many worked on bikes, visiting the homes of their usual customers to take their bets. Cosme and Marcela had tried this sales strategy to help them build clientele, but over time they realized it was more profitable simply to work out of their home.

While Marcela greeted customers, taking their bets and charging them, Cosme watched television. The procedure was too complicated for him, so he preferred to let his wife handle things. Marcela used handmade spreadsheets and a plastic jar to record the bets with the tickets. She kept the money from the bets in a dented old black tin box. The operational center of the business, where she did the numbers, checked the receipts, and set aside the money, was the dining-room table.

"It's no easy job," said Marcela, who never took her eyes off the numbers during our conversation.

The spreadsheet had eight columns and was drawn on a plain white sheet of paper. At the top of the sheet were the names of the official lotteries they offered. Customers could play the national lottery, the lottery of the province of Buenos Aires, a Uruguayan lottery called Oro, and several others. All the bets and their combinations were recorded in the rows, noting whether the customer played the same numbers in several different games. Marcela carefully wrote down the quantity and the amount bet in each of the boxes.

"If I make a mistake and someone plays a winning number, I've got a problem," Marcela explained. "The secret to this business is keeping a clean record with no mistakes." Record-keeping was made easier, however, because most of the customers played the same numbers every day, many betting on their favorite numbers on different games over the course of the day.

Besides the fact that these were brief transactions, people generally bet only a little, usually one or two pesos on each game. This was an amount shaped to an economy of marginal earnings, to people with low and irregular incomes, as described in the case of the economies of the poor in Africa by Jane Guyer (2004).

The people would come to Cosme and Marcela's house and tell them what number they wanted to play and in which game. Then they stuck their hands through the barred window to hand over the money. Marcela took the money and wrote down the bet, sometimes standing at the barred window and sometimes back at the dining-room table. All of this while drinking *mate* or coffee with Cosme and keeping an eye on the street in case a chance player or a regular came by.

A *quinielero* needs to observe two clear rules to win in the numbers game. The first is, never give credit. "If I sell on credit, I'm already in the red," Marcela insisted. Like Marga, she was exposed to the demands of customers and neighbors for credit. What distinguished the two was that the money that Marcela handled was not her own; it belonged to her boss. Both the money *earned* in these illegal transactions as well as her involvement in a network of underground trade depended on her dealings with the boss. She was just another intermediary in the pyramidal network that organized the numbers game in the neighborhood. At the end of each day, she had to report all the money that had passed through her hands to her boss. Her earnings depended on the daily balance sheet, that is, she earned the money received from the bets minus the boss's cut.

Marcela did not consider herself independent because of the money she *earned*. Being dependent on her boss was part of the moral sphere of earnings in which she moved. Being recognized by the boss as trustworthy provided moral capital that guaranteed Marcela's place in this illegal economic circuit. As it circulated, this piece of money *earned* created obligations and a special relationship to her boss. Being safe from the police was as important as the daily balance sheet that she had to present to the man providing this protection. Marcela's expectations of earnings were internally shaped by a mix of thoughts and feelings in a moral space that treated earnings obtained in underground trade as licit.

"Winners get paid immediately" is the second rule a *quinielero* must follow. There is another key here to understanding the conflict over one's moral worth. This piece of money *earned* circulates and arouses feelings and thoughts about the boss but also about customers. Marcela and Cosme's moral standing as dealers similarly depended on their immediately paying up when a bettor won: "If someone plays, they want to get paid pronto," Marcela said, showing off her expertise.

The rhythm of money circulation can be critical to having one's moral virtues acknowledged. The speedy payment to winners of the numbers game starkly contrasts with the slowness valued in requesting the return of money *lent* in other merchant-customer relations, as seen in the case of *fiado*.[5]

"I pay at once. In fact, sometimes I even go visit them to let them know they've won. That's why I have so many customers," explained Marcela. Paying quickly was the premise of her business.

A speedy circulation of money consolidated Marcela as the dealer of choice among the regulars who came in to make their bets every day. Immediate payment is key to *quinieleros'* winning their clientele's trust. By paying quickly, Marcela and Cosme proved they were reliable. However, this also depended on the boss's support. The fact was, the boss was the one who provided the prize money if someone won big.

The moral reputation of underground markets can become more demanding than that of legal markets because interpersonal relations supersede the law. The possession of moral capital can thus be the most critical factor for getting a foot in the door of these circuits and operating there. This has been shown in the literature (Beckert and Wehinger 2012), and Cosme and Marcela could attest to this.

Stolen Goods

In November 2008, I ran into "El Loco" Peralta at the parish church and he invited me to his house. There was nothing odd about that except the reason for the invitation.

"I want you to see how business opportunities just appear out of no-where. You'll see how people come looking for action, to buy or sell drugs."

I wasn't sure whether to accept, but finally I did. We walked about half a block down a street on the very edge of Villa Olimpia. A pile of rubbish served as a bridge when we needed to cross a ditch filled with stagnant water.

We reached a house in shambles. It had once been a home, and had been partially torn down by the bulldozers in the course of urbanization. You could still make out the divisions between the rooms.

These houses create fear in the neighborhood, because young people gather there to smoke the drug that worries mothers in the neighborhood the most, *paco*. What happens at these marginal spots within the slum, sites excluded from the progress of urbanization, is often exaggerated to the point of urban myth.

Peralta settled into a broken old armchair and asked me to sit next to him. He wanted to show off his power, wanted me to see he was a force to be reckoned with. He teased me, clearly aware of my discomfort.

The sound of a television could be heard from the only actual room left in the building. Peralta's cousin emerged, half dressed, and greeted him. He ignored me. Another two young men were cooking something up to add to the pot of noodles that Peralta had brought from the parish church. One of them was his brother, but they didn't seem to get along very well. The other sat down with us and started telling Peralta what he had done the previous night.

"I was at the McDonald's in San Justo."

"Got anything to sell?"

"A few cell phones."

They had clearly been stolen. Peralta, acting with authority, asked a few other questions, like what his cousin had done that day.

"Does he work for you?" I whispered to him.

"Don't say that—he'll get angry."

Nevertheless, I noticed that he was pleased that I thought he was the employer. They continued their conversation.

"So who do you think will be the first to come?" asked the young one.

"At about two, they'll all be here," Peralta told me. "That's what time the *volada* starts—when they start smoking *paco*."

None of this had ever occurred to me on the morning when I met "El Loco" Peralta in the parish church. His sister, who worked as a server at the soup kitchen at lunchtime, had introduced him to me. He had come to grab a bite and share some news: he had found a job. She asked him who had gotten the job for him, and he curtly replied that he had found it on his own. But his sister kept insisting, and finally Peralta admitted, "I have to be at Salcedo's house at eight a.m."

However, the job the neighborhood leader had offered him—cutting trees—never came through. According to Peralta, they had given him an advance and asked him to accompany the political group on marches to support the government. In greater Buenos Aires (Kessler 2002), and the slums of Rio de Janeiro (Goldstein 2003)—but also on the outskirts of Paris (Mauger 2006) and in East Harlem, New York (Bourgois 2003)—the material and symbolic disruption of the job market for poor youth has reduced the distinction between legal and illegal. Peralta had more opportunities for earning money within the underground economy than he would if he responded to *political* money.

Although the shadow economy is nothing new in neighborhoods like Villa Olimpia, the Peralta case illustrates certain transformations in the world of crime. Over the past few years, the rules of this economy have changed drastically. Gabriel Kessler refers to the traditional rule of never robbing a neighbor as "a code that permitted professionals [thieves], neighbors and police to coexist in harmony. . . . Drugs, however, justify breaking the rule" (Kessler 2002). In Villa Olimpia, the spread of *paco* configured a new stage in the underground economy and transformed the relationship of neighborhood life with crime.

"I was on the streets for around sixteen years," Santiago, a member of the last generation to observe the codes of crime, admitted. "I never robbed here in the neighborhood—I always went to other neighborhoods, downtown. Now everything's changed. You come here and the kids on the block are waiting for you at the entry point to steal whatever you've got."

When I met Santiago in November 2008, he was thirty-five. He had retired from robbery and worked in construction. "I started working in 2003. That was the first time I had ever actually had a job. . . . Two years, from the time I was sixteen until I was eighteen, but then I went out on my own. I went to prison four times, did about five years. Then I got tired of all that so I found work in construction. Salcedo came to me and asked me if I wanted a job. It was hard to get used to, but I managed."

For Santiago, the changes in the economy of crime were as important as the new job opportunities associated with urbanization:

> A lot of criminals have left the neighborhood now, and those who don't work are just idiots. Because there's plenty of work. And crime's not like it used to be, because there used to be someone to show the kids just getting into it how things worked. Ever since base paste turned up, these punks do idiotic things like robbing the neighbors, robbing people waiting for the bus. . . . The whole drug thing changed everything. The guy who used to do coke now does *paco*. Things are bad in the slum. I'm surprised they haven't robbed you yet.

Santiago's telling establishes a before and after in terms of criminal codes and the drug trade in Villa Olimpia. The relationship between thieving as a living and neighborhood relations changed when base paste addicts began robbing their neighbors: the stealing started and ended in the neighborhood and the stolen objects were generally sold to local residents.

That's what happened with the washer, gas canister, and tennis shoes stolen from Mary's house. The day after the robbery, as we walked through the neighborhood, she mentioned it to everyone she knew, asking if they had heard anything. Many of them were tied to illicit trade—perhaps one of them was behind the crime—but they all just shook their heads. A month later, she recovered the washer, because she found out that a friend of a friend had purchased it in the neighborhood. She herself had bought a dog for twenty pesos; some time later, she found out the dog was stolen. The owner, who also lived in the neighborhood, demanded she return it.

In addition to this circulation of objects robbed and resold right in the neighborhood and associated with *paco* smoking, there was the circulation of goods that the *chorros* (thieves) stole from other neighborhoods. Mary was proud of a state-of-the-art television that she had purchased for around a thousand pesos. A friend of hers, then in jail, had stolen it from a summer house in a more well-to-do neighborhood in greater Buenos Aires. According to Mary, her friend was one of the old-school *chorros* who respected the codes of the neighborhood.

Unlike Santiago and Mary's friend, Peralta was part of a new generation that smoked *paco*. He had no problem robbing in his own neighborhood.

My fieldwork in Villa Olimpia outlines Peralta's role in the new economy of neighborhood crime. One day, as I was talking with Luciana from the window of the Caritas office, she kept her eyes on a house with red gates that Peralta was eying. "I think he wants to rob Romeo's house," she said. I looked over and saw him stretch his arm through the gates and take hold of something on the other side. "I'm going to tell Sonia. She knows Romeo. He has to keep an eye out for Peralta," said Luciana before turning to leave.

A few days later, a young man from the neighborhood said he knew Peralta. He referred to him as a *pastabasero* (a base paster). "Everyone in the neighborhood knows who he is. He's a scumbag, a shoplifter. He takes whatever he can. He torments people."

On that day he had taken me to show me the business, in the rundown armchair, Peralta had tried to present himself as a small dealer in an underground market, someone who knew the rules and the risks. He referred to himself as a businessman, "I don't rob any more—I'm a businessman." And the sale of stolen goods was one of the activities that Peralta associated with this role. So was the purchase of drugs by people from other neighborhoods or by the residents of Villa Olimpia who crossed the ditch so that their neighbors wouldn't see them. However, by referring to illegal transactions as business, he portrayed himself as an upstanding citizen in the neighborhood economy, making his earnings morally legitimate.

In his ethnography on dealers in the *banlieues* (suburbs) of French cities, Thomas Sauvadet (2006) invites us to deconstruct the idea of "easy money" that is sustained inside and outside these networks. Like Sauvadet's informants, Peralta thought that easy money came to him.

"Five pesos are waiting for me on the corner," he said to me jokingly.

"And where do you get the money from?"

"Oh anywhere. Money comes easy to me. Sometimes I am sitting at home and it just comes—I'm lucky that way. Check this out: when it's for drugs, there's always money, but when it's to buy bread, no one shows up, you can't get any . . . That bag, how much is it worth? And what about that phone in your pocket? You know how much I could get for that?"

In spite of his notion of earnings, Peralta didn't think it was so easy to make a living. The money *earned* through theft involved building a moral reputation with his neighbors-customers. The sources of the money *earned* by Peralta included the sale of stolen cell phones. Without a moral space of earnings constantly under construction, these transactions would not allow Peralta to access what he considered easy money.

In November 2008, at Liliana's house, two young women named Marcia and Naty shared a *mate* with me. We talked about the parish church and other neighborhood topics. Marcia had a bit of gossip: "Ana bought a cell phone with a camera for sixty pesos."

"Ana is a neighbor who lives off welfare," Liliana clarified for my sake. "She's got eight kids and they're always dirty and wearing rags. One day her husband walked out, left her to fend for herself. I can't understand how she could spend money on a cell phone."

Marcia took out her own phone.

"I bought this pawned for sixty pesos."

"I bought mine pawned for sixty pesos too—and in installments," Liliana added.

She saw my expression of disbelief.

"Ariel, you know about pawning, right?"

Playing along, I said I didn't. Marcia proceeded to give me a lesson on the purchase and sale of stolen cell phones.

"All these kids are out stealing phones. Like Peralta. Last weekend, they were at it all day. They bring you a cell phone or something else and they say they'll sell it for sixty pesos. You say it's too much and offer them thirty or twenty. So then, since they need the money because they're jonesing [i.e., craving *paco*], they agree. But they're actually pawning it to you: you give them thirty pesos, but if they come back within a certain time, they give you back your thirty pesos and you have to give them back the cell phone. So let's say you offer him thirty: the kid says to you, 'I'll come reclaim it by seven p.m. tomorrow.'"

"So if he comes back before seven with the money, you have to give it back," I respond.

"Yes, because that means he found a better buyer, someone willing to pay sixty. But if he shows up one hour or one minute after the agreed time, you don't give it back. Since these are kids from the neighborhood, we all know them, and if you buy their items once, they'll show up at your house. 'You there, lady?' they'll call out and when you appear, they've got all sorts of stuff to offer. They put together a clientele."

In these transactions, the obligations of both buyers and sellers were critical. The moral capital of both parties served to facilitate exchanges marked by uncertainty and outside the scope of the law. Liliana assured me that everyone respected the pawning agreements, "because everyone knows everyone here, and if they do something like give you a faulty cell phone, no one is going to buy from them anymore."

Liliana had purchased her cell phone in installments.

"I paid sixty pesos for this. First I bought it for twenty and then I kept on paying. The kids would come over to my house. 'Ma'am . . . ?' And if I had something to give them, I'd hand it over—five, three, ten pesos. So that's how I gradually paid it off. The one thing they respect is if you have a family. They knew I did, so they would never show up after midnight."

In spite of the possibility of having one's sleep interrupted, these transactions were an accepted part of family budgets. "My husband always tells me to have a little cash on hand, just in case they show up with something good," Liliana said.

The money *earned* in this transaction was left open to negotiations, as Naty noted: "When you finally pay them off, they keep on coming. 'Well ma'am . . . ?' You tell them you already paid what you owe, but they ask for a peso or two. 'Please, lady . . . just a few pesos and we won't bother you again.' And sometimes you give it to them."

"'OK, here you go,' you say and you give them a few pesos. Otherwise, you'll never get rid of them," Marcia added.

Pawning marked the start of a transaction that sellers wanted to keep open as long as possible. Not keeping track of payments does not suggest careless accounting, but instead the desire to extend earnings. The transaction cycle included the sale and the request for installments. For customers, giving more after paying off their purchase was a way to ensure the seller would offer them new things. As one local told me, "You have to be patient, because they could show up with something good." Vendors built up a clientele, and customers in turn instilled trust by assuming reciprocal obligations in the pawning relationship.

During my fieldwork, I had my own experience. I was leaving the neighborhood one day when some kids came over and offered me a laptop. The three women who had discussed pawning with me asked me how much they wanted for it. I hadn't dared to ask.

"They must have seen you at church, because they only approach people they know. One of them saw you and said, 'I saw that guy at Father Suárez's,'" Marcia explained.

When I took out my cell phone and placed it on the table, Liliana smiled and added, "You have to upgrade your phone. Now that you know all about pawning."

My obsolete cell phone was evidence that I had not yet adapted to the social ties and economic transactions that sustained the market of stolen goods in Villa Olimpia. For these women, who proudly carried around their phones, purchasing such goods was part of daily economic life.

As seen in this last story, the "decent" values of material progress often take shape through activities associated with the "code of the street." The dichotomy of decent families versus street families has little analytical value for transactions like that of the stolen cell phones. In this chapter, I propose examining them from the perspective of moral capital.

The stories of Marga, Marcela, Cosme, and "El Loco" Peralta show the dynamics of accumulating moral capital, dynamics connected with the way *earned* money circulates on the underground economy. Possessing this capital is the way into these underground economic transactions. Shadow markets are moral spaces where the legitimacy of money *earned* comes into play. To get involved in these transactions, morality is a prerequisite for participating and allows parties to be ranked on a hierarchy.

Earlier in this chapter, we saw money *earned* interacting with other pieces. These moments reveal how the puzzle assembly approach is a useful methodological tool for understanding the meanings of money in social life. With this tool, the moment when people's status and power comes into play through the assembly of different pieces of money can be put together as an ethnographic narrative. The methodological attitude is key to an analytical reconstruction of the relationship between money, morality, and power.

Moving away from market exchanges, the next chapter applies this interpretation to money *donated* to the poor by the state and other institutions.

Donated Money

3

PABLO WAS EIGHTEEN YEARS OLD. He lived with his family in a neighborhood like Villa Olimpia, another *villa miseria* where urban development is currently under way. Pablo's mother struggled to keep him in school. When she was a girl, she had to work on the sugarcane plantations in the province of Chaco. The work conditions were grueling, and she had never had a chance to study. This memory returned every time Pablo stopped going to school—she didn't want her son to end up the way she had, without a high school degree. However, Pablo wanted to help out the family, so he would take odd jobs here and there to earn money instead of attending school. In the household, the only one with a steady job was Pablo's father, but he did not earn enough for the family of five to get by. In 2010, as Martin Hornes (2014) tells it, the family's life changed. Pablo managed to stay in school and no longer took odd jobs. That year, his mother began receiving AR$220 per month from the state welfare program Asignación Universal por Hijo. This money, which they withdrew each month from an ATM close to home, was contingent upon Pablo attending school and getting regular medical check-ups. This story could represent the experience of many other families in a number of countries across the world. Conditional cash transfer (CCT) programs have become the new paradigm of the struggle against poverty.

According to the World Bank, in 1997, Brazil and Mexico were the only countries with programs of this kind; by 2008, however, conditional money transfers were being made as part of welfare benefits in fifteen countries in the region. In Brazil, nearly eleven million families benefited from these programs, and five million families in Mexico, one and a half million in Colombia, and a quarter of a million in Chile also received them. In Ecuador, 40 percent of the population is covered. These programs have progressively expanded to around thirty other countries in the region that has come to be known as the Global South. CCTs have also been implemented in the developed countries as well. In New York, for example, the program Opportunity NYC was launched in 2007. Unfortunately, it was not as successful as the programs that had inspired it, such as Bolsa Família in Brazil and Oportunidades in Mexico.[1]

In Argentina, the Asignación Universal por Hijo (AUH) program was the local version of this new program to fight poverty. On October 29, 2009, Argentine president Cristina Fernández de Kirchner signed a presidential decree to launch the AUH program. Shortly before the program's launch, I wrote an editorial entitled "Poverty and the Monopoly of Moral Representation" for the newspaper *Crítica de la Argentina*.

The article discussed the construction of moral arguments "by certain politicians who have made a career by imposing their moral values on society." In the specific case of arguments in favor of expanding the welfare state, I said that need was being turned into a virtue. "Those who talk of 'freeing' the poor through state assistance or who refer to them as 'hostages' of poverty turn their political activity into a question of the morality at stake when providing state resources to the poor for them to spend," I wrote. The political capital of the legislators was inversely proportional to the immorality that, in their opinion, corroded the social lives of the poor.

"Doesn't the widespread claim of 'arbitrary' and 'discretionary' uses of welfare money by beneficiaries suggest that a group of external actors are imposing their own set of values onto a group of people whom welfare has helped incorporate into society?" I asked. I noted that certain sociologists and anthropologists interested in issues related to the poor had offered some answers to these questions over the past few years. "It would be good to hear what scholars have to say instead of this one-sided narrative of the poor, their morality or lack thereof, and government welfare programs."

Newspaper readers with access to the Internet joined in the debate with their comments. "Sociologists and anthropologists, put down those books! They're dangerous!" wrote one. "There is an enormous difference between charity and a political boss tossing some bills around. As Eva Peron once said, behind every need is a right that has been violated."

"This man supports the government!" complained another. "Instead of discussing morality, maybe he should ask what happens when the poor look at a state subsidy as an incentive to keep on having children. Mr. Wilkis, if you're a sociologist, shouldn't you be examining that side of the issue?"

Some of the comments were more aggressive. "'Arbitrary' and 'discretionary' apply to the way this corrupt administration distributes money to fund its own social movements! How can we allow the state to treat the poor like slaves? What about providing them with education, support, and protection?!"

Other responses were more conciliatory, though the contents were similar: "Ariel, it's very likely that universal welfare won't end poverty but let's be honest: discretionary distribution of welfare doesn't end poverty either and these plans are often used to obtain political sway with the poor. This universalism would serve to reduce the 'cash' that each successive administration uses to try to manipulate the poor. Let's do the math: the Tupac Amaru social organization in the north of Argentina gets ten million pesos a month. That's two hundred pesos a month for fifty thousand children."

The debate in 2009 showed how the symbolic struggles surrounding the poor had turned into a moral dispute over welfare money, as part of a broader process of redefining the role it played in the life of the poor. To understand this, it is useful to put into perspective the central importance that public money has among the most deprived segments of the poor. In 2003, a census of the inhabitants of a settlement in the county of La Matanza showed that more than half of local households (54 percent) received welfare checks, and these programs provided 36 percent of the neighborhood's income. The broadest coverage was attained when the AUH program was launched. The poverty and extreme poverty indexes had been diminishing gradually since 2003, but welfare coverage remained strong. Between 2 and

6 percent of Argentina's budget was allocated to welfare between 2002 and 2009 (Cogliandro 2010).

The reactions to the editorial are indicative of society's attitudes to the money *donated* to the poor, which instantly becomes *suspicious* money. From this perspective, the right of the underprivileged to receive social protection in the form of money becomes a topic for debate and those who voice their opinion believe that they are in a position to judge the uses of that money. In these reactions, we see people justifying why someone on welfare should or should not receive money. By doing so, they reveal their conceptions of worthiness, justice, equality, inequality, and solidarity. This piece of money thus empowers people to judge and to condemn, becoming moral entrepreneurs (Becker 1997) through money *donated*.

Given that the development experts interested in the role of CCT programs (Hanlon et al. 2010) have not explored the concept of money, power dynamics such as these have largely escaped them. This chapter contributes to expanding these perspectives, showing how power relations are formed through money relations, especially when these involve the piece I have referred to as *donated* money.

The concept of moral capital shows how *donated* money establishes a moral ranking and thus creates power relations as it circulates. On the one hand, this piece ranks those who have the power to judge along with those who are the target of such judgments. First of all, it ranks those who are judged positively in comparison to those judged negatively through access to *donated* money. From this point of view, money *donated* is a test for the poor, one in which they are subject to definitions and obliged to negotiate their moral status. This chapter narrates the production of social orders based on money that emerges from judging the life of the poor through this type of money and their attempts to keep from being downgraded (Garfinkel 1956) as the result of such biases. This exploration will allow us to see that money *donated* to the poor represents a richer and more complex reality than that which emerges from the letters to the editor of *Crítica de la Argentina* cited above.

Legitimately Donated Money

To understand the production of moral hierarchies through disputes associated with money *donated* by the state, I'll begin by reconstructing certain scenes from fieldwork I conducted before my visits to Villa Olimpia.[2] In the first case, I focused on the experiences of vendors selling a magazine produced by the homeless, and in the second, on a group of waste recyclers who live in neighborhoods similar to Villa Olimpia but whose work takes them to middle-class neighborhoods.

It was 2001. Argentina had been suffering a terrible economic recession for three years. Social and urban borders had been transformed in patterns similar to other major Latin American cities (Schapira 2002; Janoschka 2002). Like other capitals across Latin America—Quito, Lima, Montevideo, Mexico City, Santiago—Buenos Aires was also a fragmented city at the start of the twenty-first century. The processes of segregation, from both above (new gated communities, high-security apartment towers) and below (new slums, properties overtaken by squatters, and other peripheral settlements), also sketched new borders. To use Erving Goffman's term, there were countless examples of "mixed contacts": people from different social classes in close physical proximity to one another. The unemployed who live on the city's outskirts, for example, marched on the main square of Buenos Aires to demand more welfare programs. Informal workers came downtown every day—sometimes alone and sometimes with family in tow—to pick through the trash. It also became clear to the residents of the capital that an increasing number of people were living on the street.

In June 2001, I myself experienced one of those mixed contacts in a broken city. A vendor of the local magazine published by the homeless, *Hecho en Buenos Aires*, offered me his product. It was a version of the pioneering British publication *The Big Issue*: a handful of pages with a few interesting articles and classifieds. The vendor told me that he was trying to earn enough money to get off the street by selling the magazine.[3] After reading it, I wrote a letter to its editor, saying: "I am sending you this e-mail to congratulate the entire editorial staff on this initiative to resist exclusion and seek out alternatives for survival. I believe that in the times we live in, the only way to fight injustice and inequality is to work together to find creative solutions."

Other readers who sent letters to the editor hinted at a tacit understanding of what was going on with us educated middle-class men and women with a certain concern for social issues, in encounters with the magazine's vendors. These letters minimize the discomfort of such unequal meetings and instead highlight the gratification and happiness they bring. In issue 29, a letter to the editor read: "I heard about you on *La Misión* [a television program]. I was moved by your impressive work so I hit the streets to look for you and I was finally able to purchase the magazine." Later, in issue 38, someone wrote:

> One day I found a woman sitting on my doorstep. It was a meeting with a kindred spirit; she was selling *Hecho en Buenos Aires*. I learned a lot from talking to her. I think the most important lesson was about life's uncertainty. . . . One person has a house, another is on the street, but nothing is set in stone. Now I am happy whenever I run into someone selling the magazine and I always go over to talk with them.

The French sociologist Isaac Joseph believes that these street magazines have altered the face-to-face experience with homeless people. They are still "others," but less so: their otherness has been reduced. They circulate among us and come over to speak with us, giving us a personal contact with the vendor, that surprising moment referred to in these letters. Those who write try to convey the emotions and effects that the experience imparted.

Could these emotions still be expressed if we removed the money given to the vendor from the buyer? The feelings expressed in these letters play a critical role in this chapter, showing the opinions and feelings associated with a legitimate piece of *donated* money.

The Face of Money

Diego had had a bad night. His entire face was covered with bruises. He didn't remember much—only that the previous day, September 7, 2004, had been his birthday, and that he had sold every copy of *Hecho en Buenos Aires* that he had with him.[4] Later he drank too much. "I got drunk and I guess I got into a fight—I don't even know what happened," he said. "I'm not even sure where I slept, but I can tell you it wasn't in a bed and it wasn't under any roof. . . . What I do know is that I can't go out and sell the magazine looking like this."

From Georg Simmel to Marcel Mauss, and later Erving Goffman, sociologists have intuitively recognized the face's value to maintain or dissolve social bonds.[5] "What is deepest is the skin," Gilles Deleuze says, which is especially true in spaces like the street, and vision is our most developed sense, according to Simmel. On the street, then, face value becomes particularly important. Diego may not have been able to explain why, but he knew he could not go out to sell the magazine until his face healed.

Returning to the letters to the editor, we can see how money plays a prominent role in the exchanges between vendor and buyer. In *Hecho en Buenos Aires* no. 12, a woman writes: "I went over to a vendor and asked him for a copy, paying with a two peso bill; when he told me he didn't have change, I suggested he keep the change. The vendor handed me another copy and said, 'You know what, how about taking another copy and giving it to a friend?' It was then that I understood the most important part about the magazine: to give their work meaning again." For the woman, the fact that the vendor would not accept her charity was an important gesture, one which reaffirmed the nature of the sales transaction. It was not what she had expected. She discovered that the vendor had to sell to make his money, and that the magazine had given meaning back to his work.

These testimonies reveal the feelings and perspectives that give a specific form to the money that connects buyers and sellers. This connection clearly assumes an identity if we consider a passerby's reaction when a person on the streets asks for it. The set of feelings and perspectives associated with these interactions generally corresponds to *suspicious* money, though other pieces may come into play. There are three possible responses to a beggar's request for money: never give money, give once in a while, or always give, generally to the same person (Damon 2002). In all three, *suspicious* money generally prevails in such encounters.

On the one hand, money grants independence, since it can always become something else (Simmel 1900). More recent perspectives, like Viviana

Zelizer's sociology of money, add some limitations, such as social, cultural, and moral restrictions associated with the use of money. On the other hand, in these fleeting interactions, the request for money offers no guarantees as to how the money will be used. It is no coincidence that when people ask for money on the street, the most common substitute tendered is food. This type of good is given instead of money to diminish a twofold suspicion that encompasses both the freedom money grants and the intent of the person who is asking for it. Replacing the money with food reduces uncertainty about the use of the money because the money is not placed in the hands of the beggars and because the food guarantees that the donation covers a need.

The case of *Hecho en Buenos Aires* shows that the set of feelings and per-spectives of *suspicious* money can be challenged and reassembled, giving way to other meanings. Nearly all of the magazine's vendors had to answer the question, "How did you end up on the street?" But since they were now selling instead of begging, it seemed like a legitimate question, and each vendor chose a way to tell his or her life story.

Vendors were expected to give real evidence of their social identity (Fas-sin 2000). And this face-to-face contact altered many buyers' prior opin-ions about homeless people. "I wanted to tell you that when I bought the magazine for the first time, I understood how your whole perspective can change once you start to get to know people," a woman wrote in no. 32 of the magazine. Originally she had thought that people were living on the street because they wanted to do so, but her encounter with a vendor disabused her of this notion: "The man who sold me the magazine was very courte-ous and friendly," she added, "and he told me that he hadn't had other job opportunities in his life. . . . Now I know that people are not on the street because they want to be there."

In no. 21, a reader notes the signs of how that other person from the street takes cares of himself, a care he had never imagined before and which influenced his opinions and his feelings. "I had the opportunity to meet an *HBA* vendor," he wrote. "Seeing him made me as happy as running into a friend whom you haven't seen in some time. I was moved hearing this man proudly tell me about his work and about how he had turned his life around." Thanks to the combination of the story and the emotion, a specific piece of money—*donated* money—was able to circulate. However, this kind of *donated* money is free from the stigmas revealed in the responses to my editorial about cash for the poor as a state welfare benefit. The authors of those letters to the editor regarded money *donated* by the government as *suspicious*.

In the case of those purchasing the magazine, money *donated* served to acknowledge someone's effort, to compensate someone for trying, to differentiate or rank the vendor in comparison to those who tried to obtain money in other ways, such as begging, or those who used the money for other things, like buying drugs or alcohol. The expectations, emotions, and classifications associated with the social identity of the vendors were anchored in their obligation to take care of themselves.

People expected the vendors to have a certain face, one suitable for the currency that circulated between themselves and the buyers. The public performance of one's appearance was the source of the moral capital of those selling the magazine. *Donated* money could only come the vendors' way if they were capable of a public performance that guaranteed acknowledgment of their moral virtues.

This is why Diego couldn't go out to sell *Hecho en Buenos Aires* the day after the fight. With his face swollen and bruised, would he elicit that positive surprise, that happy feeling in the buyer? Could he inspire congratulatory letters to the editor? The bruises left Diego out of a public performance centered on taking care of himself. They definitively excluded him from the set of positive feelings and perspectives—free from stigmas—sometimes associated with *donated* money. And if he hit the street with a pile of magazines, he was at risk of eliciting the set of feelings and perspectives associated with *suspicious* money.

Money Not Donated

In 2001 and 2002, trash picking increased exponentially as a result of the high level of unemployment and the sudden devaluation of the Argentine peso (Paiva and Perelman 2008). According to estimates, around a hundred thousand people in the city of Buenos Aires and its outlying suburbs resorted to picking over trash at that time to survive. Those who adopted this old practice were now referred to as *cartoneros*, though all the major cities in Latin America had their own word for trash pickers: *desechables* in Colombia, *catadores* in Brazil, *chamberos* in Ecuador, *buzos* in Costa Rica, and *pepenadores* in Mexico. It is an endeavor fraught with social stigma.

In 2006, a group of about twelve *cartoneros* launched a project to recycle trash picked up in the town of Rufino in the province of Buenos Aires. I came into contact with their co-op as a member of a team of anthropologists, sociologists, biologists, and graphic designers collaborating to put together the program Reciclando Basura, Recuperamos Trabajo (Recycling Trash, Creating Jobs). In 2006, a law was passed on solid urban waste in the province of Buenos Aires decreeing that it would "gradually incorporate household waste separation, reuse and recycling by the municipalities." Each municipality was to be responsible for incorporating informal collection and recovery into its integral waste pickup plan. The Basura Cero (Zero Waste) program was implemented by the government of the province of Buenos Aires pursuant to this legislation. As a result of this program, the co-op received the support of the local government.

Most of them came from the most infamous neighborhoods of La Matanza,[6] slums and settlements a few kilometers from Rufino. The majority were already picking through trash on their own, earning a meager living at the bottom of the retail chain by selling miniscule amounts of different materials for pennies. The oldest among them had worked at a trade (e.g., as builders or drivers) in the past, while the youngest ones had only picked over trash and done odd jobs here and there.

The members of the co-op came from notorious neighborhoods, associated with danger and crime. How could they build up the trust necessary to be able to visit homes two or three times a week to pick up recyclables? Moreover, in Rufino, horse-drawn carts, driven by either adults or children, has been a common sight since the height of the crisis in 2001. The contact between these *carreros* (cart people) and Rufino residents was minimal, and usually involved them hauling away trash piled up in front of houses, such as fallen branches or builders' waste.[7] There were rumors, too, that the *carreros* were responsible for the rise in crime in Rufino. Residents began to rally to keep these horse carts from passing through the neighborhood, and in some cases, drivers were asked to show the contents of their carts every time they entered or exited it.

The beliefs about those who came from other places and, worse, were associated with trash pickup created a bias that the co-op had to contend with at every turn. This is how I saw Santiago do so in November 2006: "Hello ma'am, we're from the co-op," he said simply. "We come by between ten and twelve. If you have any cardboard, newspapers, plastic, or glass bottles, could you set them aside for me on Thursday? And leave them out there?" He pointed to a spot a safe distance from the doorway.

The collectors started wearing vests and hats with the logos of the co-op and of their program, "Recycling trash, creating jobs." Besides covering up their dirty, worn-out clothing, this uniform also contributed to the idea that they were providing a service to the neighborhood. They carried credentials with their names and identification numbers, and the phone numbers of both the co-op and the Rufino municipality.

The idea of a service was emphasized by the fact that collectors all pushed the same carts, specially designed for this pilot operation. They also handed out glossy flyers to explain the reasons for the initiative and provide logistical information (the streets the collectors visited each day of the week, a list of materials they could pick up, etc.). The goal was for residents to distinguish the co-op workers from the *carreros* and their negative image, who also circulated in the neighborhood in search of cardboard and plastic in the trash.

The collectors had to make a concerted effort for the neighbors to remember on what days they came by. They also had to deal with the risk of *carreros* or a private firm hired by the municipal government getting to the waste first. After a time, they had perfected their schedule and routes. They knew which houses left things for them and which did not; they knew which neighbor, besides setting things aside for them, would offer them something to eat or drink; they knew who liked to chat with them when they picked up the trash.

I walked down the streets of Rufino with Martín. He knew the neighborhood by heart, including which houses set aside recyclables. I noticed that certain residents came out to hand over their materials, while others left them in a bag tied onto a tree branch out front.

Another co-op worker, Lito, had a similar agreement with the residents. The first time I went out with him on his route and saw him walk through the front gate of a home or onto the lawn or porch to pick up the recyclable trash, I was struck by how comfortable he was entering private property.

The co-op's collectors kept to a schedule, unlike the *carreros*, who were unpopular in the neighborhood because of their unpredictability. By establishing a schedule and keeping to it, the co-op created a serious image of itself, and residents in turn tried to keep the waste flowing in their direction and not to the *carreros*.

The positive image of regularity and professionalism was not the only factor in the moral acknowledgment of the co-op workers. One afternoon, as I accompanied Lito on his rounds, I discovered another factor in a brief exchange with a local woman:

"I always put things aside for them. It's giving them work, after all. Plus, the *carreros* can be a little threatening."

"What do you mean by threatening?" I asked.

"They ask you for other things and force you into it. They ask for money. They say, 'Lady, we always come by to pick up your stuff.' These gentlemen are dependable," she continued, pointing at Lito, "Not like those boys who think that because they take your trash they can ask you for money and give you a dirty look if you say no. Those people are here to beg. And then they get used to begging. Now these men, they come, pick up your stuff, and that's that. They're always clean. It's a whole other deal. It's work. They don't just take your trash and then dump it elsewhere, like the *carreros*."

The woman's comments revealed that money was not expected to circulate among the collectors. The flyer handed out to each neighbor summarized this clearly: "The members of our co-op are not asking for money, only for materials that will later be recycled."

The moral capital of the Rufino collectors' co-op increased as moral antagonism with the *carreros* intensified. The more the co-op collectors were able to distinguish themselves from the *carreros*, the more moral capital they accumulated. If the distinction between the two became blurry, the recyclables would be handed over to either indiscriminately, and the symbolic differences between the two groups would be erased. It didn't matter that both the co-op collectors and the *carreros* shared the same social conditions—

the trash business, marginalized neighborhoods, mixed family and political networks—the co-op collectors stood out from the *carreros* because they were organized, tidy, and never asked for handouts.

When the trash recovery project began, I came into contact with the women of Caritas at the Rufino parish church. Caritas is one of many secular groups in Argentina that channel the social assistance provided by the Catholic Church. The role of the organization became more visible as poverty grew and the state delegated palliative measures to these civil organizations. When they had time to do so, the women had met at parent meetings at the private Catholic school their children attended in Rufino. Every month, they handed out bags of food to approximately 140 women. During our discussions, they shared their views on volunteering and their dedication to helping the needy.

When I accompanied one of the recyclers, Lito, to pick up Mabel's waste, this resident shared her impressions of the recyclers who worked the streets of Rufino with us. She emphasized money's part in the transactions. "We hope that it'll be a positive experience. I mean, people tend to be distrustful. . . . It's not like these are their neighbors. In this country, no one can be trusted unless they show a credential. But I started separating the trash to lend a hand. It's a job of some sort. After all, if they're earning money, at least they're not on welfare or out stealing."

These stories allow us to see how money seeps into the moral capital of the collectors. The co-op workers were recognized because their public performance during their visits to the neighborhood and exchanges with the neighbors excluded the money associated with the *carreros*. Asking for handouts, a special kind of *donated* money, was not part of this performance. But the money *donated* by the state (e.g., welfare) was also excluded, because for Mabel—and for the authors of the letters to the editor of *Crítica de la Argentina*—this was embarrassingly equivalent to money *stolen*. The co-op workers could associate their activity with money *earned* through work and thus elude the stigmas generally associated with *donated* money.

This dynamic came into focus at a critical moment for the Rufino collectors.

At the end of March 2008, the co-op was facing serious financial difficulties, which led to regular arguments among its members. Members were now receiving two hundred pesos every two weeks instead of the three hundred originally agreed on, and the cutback was evident in everyone's general attitude.

In addition, members were unhappy about not being able to receive money from the neighbors. It was an unspoken fact that the collectors could reach agreements on paid work with the people of Rufino, such as removing rubble for ten pesos.

"There's work on the streets but we can't take advantage of it because they think we're going to ask for money to pick up the garbage. That's why I keep my mouth shut when I pick up something," Martín told me. He was expressing the unspoken need to exclude cash from the transaction with the Rufino residents. Why couldn't money be involved in work that was ultimately about earning money?

The anthropologist Annette Weiner (1992) came up with the formula "keeping while giving" to distinguish between goods that can be given and those that cannot. This difference establishes a hierarchy and then projects it onto people who relate to one another through such goods. Not all of social life can be encoded through goods given, received, and returned. People also construct their ties and attribute meaning to hierarchies through goods that do not circulate. The co-op collectors constructed their moral capital through money withheld from circulation.

Monetary Interactions

"What's happening is just terrible," the Caritas volunteer Mabel told me one of the days I accompanied Lito to pick up the recyclables from her house. She wasn't referring to the hot sun, which we tried to shield ourselves from by standing in the shade under her porch roof. "Yesterday the people marching on Plaza de Mayo had signs that said, 'We're not here for money.' It's different with Sánchez—he convinces people to march with him by paying them or giving them things. He wants women and children with him so that he won't get beat up."

Neither Lito nor I responded. The march had occurred in a political climate marked by an unprecedented conflict between the government and

farmers that had become known as the *conflicto del campo*.[8] Mabel identified with those carrying the signs, those who weren't there for the money,
those who stood against the government and its allies. On the opposite side
was Mario Sánchez, whose political career had started in the 1980s when
he led land takeovers and started informal settlements. Later, he had become a leader of the unemployed workers movements in the mid-1990s,
rallying against the negative consequences of neoliberalism. Sánchez, one of
the most visible faces of the *piqueteros* (protestors who blocked roads at the
start of the millennium, bringing commerce in La Matanza to a standstill),
was supporting the government in its dispute with farmers and livestock
producers.

Mabel was also expressing the ideas and feelings expressed in those
letters to the editor of *Crítica de la Argentina*. She was against the money
donated by the state and considered that welfare recipients were being ma-
nipulated by political leaders. This *donated* money was worthy of suspicion.
The well-known patronage system served as a framework for these negative
moral judgments. Yet there was an important difference between the letters
and Mabel's reaction, as hers was directed at someone who could be dis-
criminated against for receiving this money *donated* by the state.

As Mabel spoke, I wondered whether she knew that Lito had been a
member of the unemployed workers movement. He had attended rallies
of this kind in exchange for a meal or a stipend and, far from criticizing
Sánchez, he was impressed by the latter's approach to people, things, and
especially to money.

"I was on the Route 3 roadblock," Lito had told me once. "The wife of my
sister-in-law's son is with Sánchez. She's his secretary. She asked if I wanted
to participate in exchange for a [welfare] plan. We did a lot of marching back
then, when I didn't have a job."

"And what happened to your welfare when you joined the co-op? Did
you keep it?"

"I struck a deal with one of the contacts. She agreed to let me stay
on if I paid her twenty pesos. Your ability to bargain depends on your
job. The contact knows all of us and she knows where we work. Some
of them ask for seventy-five pesos to let you stay on welfare. . . . I heard
that Sánchez is going to organize recycling co-ops. I am going to go have

a word with him, because I bet he'll be getting more kickbacks from the government."

Outside Mabel's house, I wondered if Lito cared what Mabel thought. Maybe he preferred to remain quiet to avoid an argument.

Later on, beneath the Rufino bridge (the meeting point for collectors finishing their routes, where the truck picked up the bags), Sánchez came up again. However, since those participating in the discussion were peers this time—all co-op members—everyone was free to speak his mind.

"Rubio, I saw you with Sánchez at Plaza de Mayo," said Mariano in a mocking tone.

Rubio didn't like that one bit.

"That Sánchez is one son of a bitch. I went to ask him for food and he wouldn't give me any, while I watched him hand it out to guys with cars, guys with nice houses. You know what he said to me? 'Sorry, I can't give you any—it's for the group members.' I was pushing a cart and they had cars. They kept it all in that house of theirs."

This time, Lito intervened.

"Sánchez let me stay on welfare. I know him, he's my neighbor. When I had a problem with my benefits, I went to talk to him and he fixed it for me."

"El Petiso" wasn't as pleased with Sánchez.

"I was on welfare through Sánchez,[9] but once my check wasn't on the roster and they couldn't find it. Then Soledad managed to find the check—it had been sent to another office—and she offered to handle my benefits for me. She knows all the things I've been through, what with my mother and other relatives dying. I was even a polling official when Quiroga ran for city councilman!"

The Sánchez dossier was a story of a political leader and his followers, one marked by both allegiance and betrayals.

These two different scenes at the house of the volunteer and beneath the bridge offer a more comprehensive image of this moral dispute surrounding legitimate earnings. These are framed within the heterogeneous (and often opposing) systems of feelings and perspectives about money.

Lito remained silent in response to the righteousness of the Caritas volunteer. He would not defend Sánchez in this face-to-face relationship, just as he and the other co-op workers refused to mention money in their dealings with the locals to show their moral superiority to the *carreros*. In the meeting between the Caritas volunteer and Lito, he could not voice his positive perceptions and assessments of the protest leader or his own views on money. Lito was obliged to let the volunteer express her point of view, which depended on the feelings and perspectives associated with *donated* money. Keeping her as a "customer" meant not questioning her opinions. Although he had personal experience with what she was discussing—or to put it more bluntly, she was unwittingly talking about people like him—Lito could not contradict the volunteer's perceptions about money and people.

Wasn't his individual and collective *moral capital* based on the effort to earn a living, in contrast to those who were on welfare or turned to thieving to get by? Wasn't the volunteer expressing her positive assessment of Lito in comparison to poor people who resorted to lying and begging, to the point where he might actually feel proud of what she was saying about him? Due to the obligations associated with this interaction, Lito was forced simply to let the volunteer speak her mind.

All human interactions represent a small-scale social order, according to the sociologist Erving Goffman. Like the encounters between buyers and sellers of the homeless people's magazine or between the trash collectors and Rufino residents, Mabel's description provides insight into social orders established through monetary hierarchies. In all of these cases, there is a clear perspective on the poor, who are classified and differentiated by a hierarchy of money. Approval or disapproval of the poor depends on the moral assessment of how they obtain the money.

The social order that these scenes reveal would disintegrate if different pieces of money all had the same value. There had to be some way to judge people and assign them a status in the social world. The concept of *donated* money as expressed by Mabel sheds light on the money circulating as part of state welfare (akin to *stolen* money) or the money solicited by the *carreros*. On the opposite end of the spectrum is the money *earned* through hard work.

When we left Mabel's house, there was no longer any need for Lito to remain silent or abide by the unspoken rules of his exchange with the Caritas volunteer. In the argument about Sánchez, Lito's discourse hinted at another kind of moral capital inherent in the circulation of money. Lito's assessment and perception of Sánchez were not based on what he had seen in the media, as the opinions of the Caritas volunteer were. Instead, they were based on his own personal experiences.

The Brazilian anthropologist Lygia Sigaud (1996) proposed the idea that the actions, feelings, and perspectives of political or union leaders and their followers are not based on any laws but instead on their mutual obligations and exchanges with others. Sánchez's story is proof of this.

Lito expressed his thoughts more profoundly in the conversations beneath the bridge with the other co-op members. They all discussed their personal experiences, of payment obligations that Sánchez had or had not met. In this context, Lito insisted on his close relations to the leader. Lito had responded to Rubio that Sánchez was no "son of a bitch," but rather "someone who helped me out when I was in trouble." While the Caritas volunteer viewed Sánchez as a manipulator who "paid people to march with him," Lito viewed him as someone "who gets welfare for people." El Petiso's opinion revealed less exasperation than Rubio, who repeated "He never got me on welfare" as proof of injustice. By recounting his own experience, he invoked a rule implicit to the exchanges between headmen and their followers, whose bond comes with certain obligations. From his relaxed tone, it was clear that he had always acted in compliance with the rules that govern such relationships.

When we left the home of the Caritas volunteer, another layout of social order, monetary hierarchy, and status was configured, one that did not fall within the set of feelings and perspectives associated with *donated* money. Another type—*political* money—expresses it more succinctly. The analysis of these connections between pieces of money creates a more comprehensive, flexible, and realistic vision of life among the poor than the supposedly absolutist perspective.

The novel CCT programs upped the household budgets of the poor and became a focus of public debate when money *donated* by the state was used as a way to morally discredit the poor. Money *donated* to the poor instantly became a source of suspicion. To understand this, I have reconstructed the place of money *donated* by the state in different hierarchies of money. Through this reconstruction, I have shown how social orders are produced through money, allowing people to establish power and status.

The moral capital of homeless vendors selling a magazine and the members of a trash recycling co-op were evaluated here according to a monetary ranking in which money *donated* by the state is viewed as the bottom of the ladder. Both of these groups offer a public performance that emphasizes their opposition to this piece of money and their affinity with other pieces, especially money *earned*. I identified different strategies individuals use to elude the biases associated with this type of money, such as stigma-cleansing rituals, exclusion strategies, and silence in the face of judgment. Beyond the efforts to avoid the stigma associated with *donated* money, the reconstructed scenes show how monetary hierarchies uphold power relations among those who have the authority to judge and those who must acquiesce to such biases.

The puzzle assembly approach brings into question a stable, encapsulated, and one-sided meaning of money while searching for new pieces and fitting them together in different ways. Over the course of this chapter, we have seen all that this approach has to reveal within the sociology of money. The chapter begins with letters to the editor in response to my editorial in *Crítica de la Argentina* and ends by showing that these opinions and feelings do not take into account the new meaning that recipients of money give to it based on their own social and political ties. At the point where those who criticized my editorial saw only immorality, manipulation, and shame, sociology encounters other principles by which moral capital accumulates and money circulates. In the next chapter, I explore this *other* social order that is produced through *political* money.

Political Money

4

MAX WEBER OFFERED A LUCID ANALYSIS of money in politics. I venture that his sociology of money is an important chapter in his political sociology. For Weber, democracy and money are intertwined with political life. The competition between political parties makes money a critical part of their activities (Weber 1991 [1946]). From this perspective, money helps rationalize political life, stabilizing the relationships between leaders and followers.

During the processes of democratization in Argentina—and most of Latin America—that began at the beginning of the 1980s, political scientists and sociologists began examining money in political life through the finances of political parties (Zuleta Puceiro et al. 1990), corruption (O'Donnell 1993), and political clientelism (Auyero 2001; Calvo and Murillo 2004; Vommaro 2010). This perspective, like Weber's, attributes an instrumental role to money in political life. Money is presented here as a means to organize political parties, achieve electoral support, and obtain extralegal benefits.

This instrumental narrative of money in politics is not exclusive to analysts of Latin American democracies. In a classic work on political sociability in the Boston slums, *Street Corner Society* (1943), W. F. White described how money circulated without damaging the bonds between political leaders and their followers. Since money was a depersonalized medium of exchange, White argued, it lacked the power to enforce moral obligations. This interpretation involves a conception of money as morally weak.

In the context of Argentina, the money that circulates in poor neighborhoods as part of political support is nothing new. The way in which political networks feed economic resources into these neighborhoods has been examined in the context of the return to democracy in the 1980s (Ossona 2014), the neoliberal reforms during the 1990s (Auyero 2001), and in Argentina's poorest provinces (Vommaro 2010). Unlike these works, which focus on contexts in which money is not essential to political exchanges, my fieldwork in Villa Olimpia gave me another perspective. The process of urbanization and Salcedo's rise as a political figure created a political market increasingly centered on the circulation of money. When Mary said that "money grows on trees here in Villa Olimpia," it was a reference to this essential role of money. When these processes are examined, several questions appear. Has the monetization of political activities dissolved values, commitments, and loyalties among the poor? Is this corruption or an ethical exchange among people who lack cash but possess moral capital? This book seeks to go beyond a narrative of money's instrumental use in politics and in this chapter specifically I am interested in exploring how politics involves power relations that can be understood through the moral dimension of money.

Money for Everyone

Analía was still passionate about Paraguay. Our conversations inevitably turned to the *danza de la botella*, a folk dance of her native country. She would proudly pull out pictures of her and her daughters, all dressed in white, with blue and red ribbons. Continuing the customs from her homeland filled her with pride; she bragged about being a great dancer and swore that she knew the secrets for making the best *chipá* and perfect *sopa paraguaya*.[1]

Like other women from Paraguay, Analía started off working as a maid at the beginning of the 1970s. Later she got a job in a textile factory. Some co-workers at the factory told her that she could buy a lot in a slum in the western district of greater Buenos Aires, and she jumped at the opportunity. With the support of her fellow Paraguayans, she built the first room of her house. However, her life in Villa Olimpia was interrupted when her father fell ill and Analía was forced to return to Asunción.

She came back fifteen years later. She had married and divorced in the interim but she again chose to settle in Buenos Aires with her four daughters. Several years would pass before she met another man, one more affectionate than her ex. He liked going out dancing with her.

During the feverish excitement surrounding the occupation in 1999, Analía was an active participant. She didn't think twice about occupying a piece of land that she divvied up with her daughters. Together they set up a tent where they slept during the long months of the occupation. As a precautionary measure, Analía almost never left them alone, especially at night. They were still young, and she was afraid of who could happen on an empty lot with no lighting.

Analía cooked for the entire group, which spent day after day on the land, never leaving. The dream of owning a home seemed well worth it. Because of her involvement in the occupation, she became part of Luis Salcedo's incipient political network. Like everyone in Villa Olimpia, she had known the future neighborhood leader since he was a boy. Analía remembered him playing soccer on the streets and working at the local bakery. Once the group had been assured they would not be evicted, Analía became a delegate. She was in charge of collecting the payments that had to be made to make the land purchases legal. The new house would be constructed with welfare funds allocated by the government. She remembers 2004 well, because it was the year the family moved into its new house.

As time passed, the slum began to experience other changes in addition to the transformations to the urban grid. The urbanization project had created new jobs associated with Salcedo's network, establishing differences among the residents. A new joke circulated in the neighborhood: "Here in Villa Olimpia, there's a 'secretary' under every stone." One day Analía went into the co-op office and handed one such secretary the money she had collected that day. When the secretary saw that she had not collected much, she tossed the wad of bills onto the desk and gestured for Analía to leave.

Analía was offended by the treatment she received. It wasn't as much a personal affront as it was a snub to the efforts of her neighbors, who had saved that money to make the installments on their future homes. She confronted Salcedo: "I'm not happy about how I was treated. I'm done here." The fact that Analía had decided to distance herself from the movement was indicative of other changes that were occurring in Villa Olimpia. She was in an ambiguous and thus painful position. As a member of the founding group of Salcedo's social network, she had bet on the leader's growth, but she had been excluded from new types of political recognition like a post as a secretary.

"It hurts, you know? I mean when push came to shove, when they [the co-op members] were going to get salaries, they didn't call me. I don't understand why they didn't call me," said Analía.

The salary was directly indicative of the transformation of the political exchanges in Villa Olimpia. She was not earning this money, clearly *political* money, in spite of all her work for the network, and this left her feeling undervalued, as if Salcedo had not acknowledged all her hard work. Distancing herself from the network avoided defeat in the struggle to accumulate moral capital.

It is useful to think of Analía's break with the network not in absolute terms but as a waiting period. Analía's day-to-day contacts still included Salcedo's people, family members, and other neighbors who were still part of the network. Things began to happen as time passed. As Analía waited, political salaries became more and more common in the neighborhood. She took note and brought it up with Salcedo every time she ran into him. "When you've got something that could work for me, let me know. I'm ready to do whatever you need."

Salcedo did in fact remember, but not the way Analía had expected. He offered to take out a loan so that she could buy a sewing machine. However, this *lent* money was clearly not the same as *political* money, though both were expressions of the moral capital that linked Salcedo and Analía. From the Paraguayan woman's position outside the network, she could obtain a loan, but in order to earn a salary, she had to prove her political virtues anew and have them acknowledged by the network. Once again, she would have to accumulate moral capital under the terms of the political exchanges between Salcedo and his followers.

At last the day arrived. On the dining-room table of Analía's house, there was a notebook with a list of the names of kids who played soccer in the neighborhood. Analía had already spoken with the local mothers, and she wanted to tell Salcedo about her project to put together a kids' soccer team.

She had been planning this for some time when she was invited to join the Villa Olimpia Sports Commission. At that point, Salcedo had spoken with the future commission members.

"There won't be a salary at the beginning but there will be eventually," he said. And then, as if to emphasize the last point, he added, "You're going to have to work hard."

Analía already had a work project laid out, and she was hoping to speak with Salcedo, to show him that she had in fact been hard at work since leaving the network. In a meeting of groups from different slums in the La Matanza area, she asked to speak in order to present her project.

"I used to be part of the co-op, but I got derailed, derailed like an old train. I went off track. I lost my way," she declared as an introduction. "But today I'm back with a whole new purpose. I want to work with kids."

In Analía's expectations, *political* money seemed a clear indicator that she was being reincorporated into Salcedo's network. Receiving this money would make her feel part of the group again, allow her to be reincorporated. This *political* money indicated that her derailed train was now back on track and rolling.

Political Competition

On our walk through the neighborhood, Salcedo explained the different steps in the urbanization process: paving streets, relocating families. His story wove together the history of the neighborhood with personal anecdotes, including his own dramatic tale. Some years back, his father had fallen ill quite suddenly and the ambulance had trouble making its way down the narrow corridors of the slum. He died before he reached the hospital. It was a tragedy that could have been avoided, like so many others in Villa Olimpia and similar neighborhoods.

"That day I said to myself, 'Enough of this. Something has to be done.'" He uttered this last phrase with anguish. The words seem to come from deep within him, though he had probably repeated them hundreds of times before.

We moved from the oldest (but still intact) sections of the slum to the line of recently constructed houses in a sort of ritual walk. As we walked, places, people, and events fell into their positions in the hierarchy. Trained to welcome outsiders—politicians, officials, students, and researchers—without question, the residents appeared to play their parts spontaneously, but the production nonetheless seemed almost planned, like a spatial representation of the neighborhood that responded to their interests. All of the residents of Villa Olimpia knew enough to understand the political value of these visits, which Salcedo's group wanted to monopolize. Those who weren't pleased with Salcedo's leadership took advantage of our public stroll to voice their discontent.

"Why don't you come see my house? It's not even close to being finished!" one man jeered as I passed by with Salcedo.

"Why don't you take him to see all the trash piled up?" another woman called out as she glared at the neighborhood leader.

Salcedo's leadership was clearly not set in stone. One of the spokespeople of the opposition to the neighborhood leader was Beto Ramírez. I heard his name several times before actually meeting him. Everyone had something to say about Beto, a seasoned Peronist activist. The Ramírez family was a political dynasty and Beto served as the family spokesperson in addition to his regular political activity. His name was painted on the walls both in Villa Olimpia and in neighborhoods nearby. Beto was in the same party as Salcedo and he was in the same political faction of Peronism in La Matanza. When career politicians had fallen out of favor around the time the urbanization process began, Ramírez's career had stalled.

Once I had won his trust, he also invited me to walk through the neighborhood with him. "I know that they showed you what they [Salcedo's group] wanted you to see. I'm going to show you the truth," he said. Ramírez sought to change the idea he believed I had formed about Villa Olimpia touring the neighborhood with his rivals. It was not only because he had seen me several times with Salcedo's cronies. It was also because of who I was—an outsider, a university researcher—which automatically put me into the category of guest on an official visit. I had to be shown an image other than the one presented by Salcedo's group. I had to "walk the neighborhood" with him.

During the walk, we met families who were angry because they still hadn't moved. We also saw new houses suffering from infrastructure issues. On our walk, the neighborhood was presented in a new configuration in which Salcedo and his group were judged negatively.

This journey through the neighborhood and the criticism of Salcedo made it perfectly clear that politicians aspiring for leading positions in the community vied for moral capital. Ramírez made me hear the voices of all those speaking out against Salcedo, most of whom attacked the leader's moral capital. Salcedo claimed to improve the lives of the Villa Olimpia residents, but these voices spoke of promises unmet and of the special privileges of Salcedo and his cronies.

The people we met along the way offered variations on the Ramírez perspective. Salcedo was criticized for affecting the political career of Ramírez and his family. It seemed as if revealing the gaps in the official story of the urbanization process was a way to rectify this situation.

"Would you like to come see the graffiti?" Ramírez asked.

He wanted me to see that he was also working hard in the feverish days leading up to the Peronist primaries.

"Salcedo's people would have you believe that I'm dead politically—but I'm alive and kicking."

His zeal whenever Salcedo's name was mentioned made it clear that he was anxious to change the balance of power.

"What do you think?"

Graffiti on walls subscribed by the Ramírez family proclaimed Salcedo's candidacy for the position of neighborhood leader. Although he protested to me that he "wasn't dead," Ramírez was reaffirming his subordination. For the time being, his political activity depended on accepting Salcedo's leadership. However, Ramírez was fearful of being totally eclipsed by Salcedo, so he wasn't sure whether to accept Salcedo's invitation to walk the neighborhood alongside the leader. If the locals saw them together, they would probably conclude that local politics now revolved exclusively around the figure of Salcedo.

Although Ramírez would try to avoid it for some time, he eventually would be forced to fall in line with Salcedo, which would mean giving up on his own political aspirations in the Peronist party in La Matanza and, more broadly, in the province of Buenos Aires. His only hope was for the following year, when co-op elections would allow him to represent those who were displeased with Salcedo. He felt sure that his political luck would change.

While he planned for a better future and thought up ways to lead the neighborhood through the transition, Ramírez paused before a few young men who were painting Salcedo's name on one of the neighborhood walls. He pointed to one of them and said: "That's exactly what I need: a guy who's earning a salary and who can be there when I need him. I'm going to talk to Salcedo to see about that, to make sure the boys who are with me get something like that, steady work."

Ramírez compared himself with Salcedo constantly, though his own career had been thwarted by Salcedo's rise as neighborhood leader. Political salaries were also a frequent point of comparison. Ramírez could not aspire to compete with Salcedo unless he could access *political* money to pay his own followers for their political support. The lack of such money diminished his moral capital as a leader. Such money would allow him to show himself to be a politician with aspirations and to express his support and recognition of followers. As we saw in the story of Analía, followers expected to receive a political salary, and their trust in a leader depended on it. Ramírez knew this was his Achilles' heel in politics and that he could not compete with Salcedo without this tool, which would allow him to be recognized as a true leader. Political salaries for his supporters would show them that Ramírez cared about them and that they could trust him—two marks of an up-and-coming politician.

The Campaign

In mid-2008, primary elections were scheduled in the province of Buenos Aires, and a campaign was organized to persuade local residents to sign on with the Peronist party. For the first time, Salcedo was going to run for a party post. Expectations were high among the members of his network.

A few months earlier, it had been hard to find Salcedo in the neighborhood (he was spending most of his time at his office in town hall), but he was now a constant presence in Villa Olimpia. His aspirations were evident in graffiti blazoning his name alongside those of other important political leaders. His presence and the intense activity of the members of his network temporarily transformed the scene in Villa Olimpia. These were weeks of nail-biting and tension, a true rite of initiation.

To meet the objective of affiliating as many residents as possible with the Peronist party, a house strategically located on the neighborhood's main street was turned into a sign-up center, so that anyone entering or leaving Villa Olimpia would have to walk past it. A photocopy machine and several computers were constantly running. The members of Salcedo's group were glued to their cell phones. Men and women passed by with their ID cards in hand. From the hustle and bustle, it was clear that the neighborhood supported Salcedo's political wager.

The party affiliation campaign was a huge success. The most optimistic of Salcedo's followers had calculated on signing up a thousand new party members. In the end, they got sixteen hundred.

"So were you signing people up for the party?" I was asked at the doorway of the parish church the week after the campaign ended. Apparently the women had spotted me in the company of one of Salcedo's supporters as she went from house to house explaining how to sign up, what documentation was needed, and most important, the repercussions that Salcedo's political career would have for the neighborhood.

The campaign left its mark. The rumors multiplied: for every affiliate a member brought in, they said, a person earned eight pesos. Other speculation followed.

I was suddenly part of the atmosphere of collective exchange created by the circulation of *political* money. I told the church ladies, "If they paid eight for every affiliate you brought in, Salcedo owes me thirty-two pesos. I brought in four!" They burst out laughing, well aware that I was an outsider in this social exchange involving politics and money. As an outsider, I was only able to evoke the feelings and perspectives related to *political* money as a parody of a very serious reality.

In the weeks following the party affiliation campaign, the church women brought up the topic again. Their jesting tone had disappeared entirely. A rumor had been spreading, later confirmed as true. "The priest found out about all the political salaries being paid. Everyone who was signing people up earned a salary." Father Francisco Suárez reacted strongly to the evidence of political salaries being paid: "I'm going to ask him to pay our people salaries as well," he told the church collaborators.

The truth was not so different from what Analía and Beto Ramírez had encountered. Father Suárez was now articulating the same thing Analía had felt when her exclusion from the network was measured in money. In fact, the priest's complaint was no different from the one Beto Ramírez was planning to present to Salcedo after the sign-up campaign: he also wanted his people to be earning salaries. Both of these men needed to get *political* money for their followers to boost their moral capital as neighborhood leaders.

A collective but also subjective transformation had taken place in the social and personal lives of many Villa Olimpia inhabitants. *Political* money had become a rampant factor in them. Analía's subjective conversion expressed a collective process at the individual level. The demands of Beto Ramírez and the priest revealed a subjective process at the social level.

In his book *The Philosophy of Money*, Georg Simmel explored the question of how money imbues social life with a generalized relationism. As its use increases, there are more opportunities for connections between people, things, situations, and social ties. The distribution of *political* money involves a process of this kind. These salaries or political payments had become part of the personal and collective life in Villa Olimpia. The opinions and the sensibilities connected to this type of money were shared by the neighborhood residents. *Political* money produced a kind of unity so strong that even a stranger had to be able to joke about it if he wanted to be involved in the collective life of the neighborhood.

Rumors

The rumors that begin to circulate deep within a group are governed by the same rules and relations that connect its members. Norbert Elias (1994) contributed to this understanding of rumors: he viewed them as indicators of a group's sociality, both because of the unity they inspire and of the competition and conflict they spark. In Villa Olimpia, the rumors about *political* money were indicative both of the new source of social unity and of the moral conflicts that were produced as it was distributed.

"So-and-so is earning a salary now—it's not a big salary, mind you, but he hardly works at all. He's going to have to work harder," a woman in Father Suárez's network told another member.

"You know that so-and-so earns regular wages for what she does?" a man asked in reference to a woman in Salcedo's group.

"I was surprised to hear that so-and-so has quit her job. I bet she and her husband are both earning a salary at the church," another man said.

"Here at the church, we don't get paid, but Salcedo did offer me a subsidy. I didn't get it through him though—I got it through another guy I know who's with another party faction. I hope Salcedo doesn't find out," a collaborator confessed.

These kinds of rumors accumulated as my visits to Villa Olimpia continued. It became increasingly clear that the social intensity of *political* money sheds light on the way agents evaluate their mutual obligations. Money becomes a moral accounting unit, displaying the earner's virtues or imperfections.

The spread of money in political exchanges transformed the way in which earners' moral obligations were evaluated, justified, represented, and fulfilled. The rumors and stories of Analía, Beto Ramírez, and Father Suárez reveal a new framework for assessing dedication in which monetary calculations are mixed with moral judgments. Money provides an objective, numerical assessment of political commitment.

The positivity of this monetary puzzle piece can be confirmed by considering how collective and individual political conversions are encouraged through *political* money: this new source of unity and moral conflict had pervaded social life in Villa Olimpia. In order to revise our concept of money in the political life of the poor, we must explore the feelings and perspectives about *political* money and discover exactly how it works—not only as compensation for tasks rendered, but also as a unit of moral accounting.

A World of Money and Obligations

When I visited Villa Olimpia for the first time, Mary and her family were living in a rickety house in the poorest area of the neighborhood: a settlement consisting of six city blocks that had been left out of the urban renovations. For this reason, the residents there felt themselves to be on the lowest rung of the social ladder. They watched with anger and sometimes envy as their neighbors—who were often relatives—gained access to more comfortable living situations.

Mary knew she had the support of the other residents of the settlement. With the help of Father Suárez, she had set up a soup kitchen. Since she had once worked as a cook, she knew how to feed a hundred children at a time. As time passed, Mary's house became the place where people came to get information, make a complaint, or solve a problem. Her family had begun playing a major role in the neighborhood even before the political changes in Villa Olimpia, but their role would become even more prominent once Mary agreed to join Salcedo's political network.

Before running for office, Salcedo had lacked the political capital he would need to control the neighborhood. The social porosity of the settlement and its marginal nature fostered rivalries among those trying to accumulate political power. Those from other groups (social movements, other factions of the Peronist party) vied for the support of locals such as Mary by promising improvements to infrastructure, new job opportunities, and contact with municipal officials.

Mary intervened on behalf of Salcedo one summer afternoon when the political disputes were as heated as the temperature. Since Salcedo was not yet a consolidated leader at that point, supporting him meant wagering on an uncertain future.

That hot day, the leader of a social movement and his followers moved to take charge of the settlement's administration. Salcedo was the first to intervene and declare he was against it; he was seconded by a few members of his still incipient network. The tension increased as the day wore on. When the argument became so intense that it looked as though physical violence might erupt, Mary interceded on Salcedo's behalf and persuaded the local residents to say that they would side with Salcedo if things turned ugly.

Mary's gesture of support worked as a sort of primitive accumulation of moral capital. Salcedo found himself confronted with someone who was wagering on his leadership, and this was irrefutable proof of her virtues, giving her the right to enter Salcedo's incipient political network, whose first members were Mary, her relatives, and some of the original members of the group that occupied the land in 1999.

After this, Mary abandoned the soup kitchen that she had organized for Father Suárez's parish. From then on, she would gear all her efforts to "supporting" Salcedo—or "working" for him, as she liked to put it.

Several years after that, I accompanied Mary to the town hall one day. She had been waiting for months on the documentation she needed in order for her Paraguayan children to become Argentine citizens. That morning, she had received a call to tell her that the paperwork was ready.

During our bus ride, Salcedo called her cell phone constantly to tell her that he was afraid a conflict would break out among residents in the settlement. He wanted to make sure she would take care of it. A young woman with several young children had occupied one of the lots without permission. She quickly managed to erect a precarious tin house there. The owner of the lot, who also lived on the settlement, had given her a deadline for abandoning the lot. Evicting a mother with children was a delicate situation. Mary intervened.

"I'm speaking on behalf of Salcedo, who is closely following the situation," she said. "We have to settle things on our own."

She spoke separately with the owner of the lot and with the young woman, and later she organized a meeting to reach an agreement. The woman would be able to stay a few more months, provided she abandoned the premises on the agreed date. Salcedo, for his part, would do everything possible to find her a lot of her own.

Mary's main job was to avoid conflict among the residents of the settlement, just as she had at that fateful meeting when she avoided strife by bringing people together behind the up-and-coming leader. She could speak "on behalf of Salcedo" as long as she remained capable of keeping everyone on the settlement in check. Her position in the network depended on it.

Stepping Down, Stepping Up

"During the presidential elections in 2003, I worked with Salcedo nonstop," Mary said. Then suddenly she added, "In the 2007 [presidential] elections, I stepped down." This was the first time Mary had ever mentioned the period when she had stopped working for Salcedo. There was clearly anger and bitterness surrounding the memory.

Mary had been sorely disappointed when Salcedo picked not her but her niece to be in charge of the settlement. In her subjective experience of what had occurred, Salcedo had neglected to acknowledge the virtues of her "political work." Stepping down meant letting Salcedo know she was upset about his decision to put her on the network's back burner. A year later, though, Salcedo reversed his decision; Mary's niece had failed as the head of the settlement's organization. Mary had been waiting for this in order to resume her previous political responsibilities.

Mary spoke negatively about Salcedo a second time after an intensive round of rallies and demonstrations that the government had organized. It was just before Children's Day. "I'm not going to take part in the celebrations," Mary said. "I don't like the way [Salcedo] has organized things." Her words took me aback. I was surprised that she wouldn't participate, after "supporting"—Mary's favorite word—all the groups from Villa Olimpia that had traveled from the neighborhood to demonstrations and rallies in support of Cristina Kirchner. She would often spend long days outside during cold weather and rain, not returning until nightfall.

Mary left me wondering: would she actually forgo an activity organized by Salcedo's group? I later realized that my surprise was due to a wrong conclusion. Mary's words reflected only the current state of her ties with Salcedo, not the broader, fluctuating cycle of mutual obligations. Her work for the leader at any given time meant that she was satisfied with what she was giving and getting from their relationship. Stepping down expressed her feeling that he was not fulfilling his obligations to her.

Mary got the settlement's residents organized and guaranteed support for Salcedo, and his recognition of her work in this regard was the source of her moral capital. For this reason, it is important to understand what had happened in the months leading up to Mary's decision to step down, that is, the political work during the rallies and what happened afterwards. Two specific moments are particularly telling, the first at Liliana's house.

"I'm off to the march," Liliana said. "Mary invited me along. She's coming to pick me up." She asked her daughter to look out the window to see whether she saw Mary.

Liliana had moved to her new house less than a year ago, but the building was already in very poor condition. For some time, there had been a horrible stench coming from a broken pipe that connected her bathroom to the sewers.

"I've got to do my part. To get them to fix the pipe in the bathroom, I have to do my part," she said.

"What does that involve?"

"Making sure they see me at the demonstration. I don't think one march will be enough to get them to fix the bathroom, so I'll go to a few more. I take my daughter with me. She likes to come along. But if Mary doesn't go, I'm not going. What would I do all alone? Look outside," she told her daughter again, "and tell me if you see her."

Liliana began to get restless at the thought of Mary not coming. "Mary said she would pick me up, but maybe she decided to sleep the *siesta* instead and she won't go because she doesn't feel like it. I'm not going on my own," she said again. Suddenly the sound of thunder could be heard not far away. "They're setting off the firecrackers. That means they're getting ready to leave."

There was still no sign of Mary, and Liliana tried to keep herself occupied by removing her nail polish. She paced back and forth through the kitchen, nervous, and then another hypothesis occurred to her. "Maybe Mary is already there with the buses."

I told her I could go over there with her but she shook her head.

"If they see me, I'll have to stay. And I'm not going by myself. . . . Plus, she invited me. She told me that she would pick me up right about now." Liliana was so anxious that she couldn't stop pacing and going over her options. Finally, she told her daughter, "Change out of those clothes. We're not going anywhere." There was a clear resignation in her words.

In the other scene, Mary was sitting in front of her house with her father and a friend. She had a list in her hand, and from time to time she looked down the street to see if anyone was coming by.

"Are you coming?" she called out to a young man who passed by the house. The man responded that he wasn't, because he'd found a job. However, he told her that his neighbor's kids would be there. Mary was fixated on her list. She was concerned about how the names were spelled, and she asked me to write them down for her.

Two hours later, in a bus heading towards the city of Buenos Aires, we reached the highway tollbooth. A long line of school buses were waiting at the booths. They hailed from different places in the province of Buenos Aires, and all were clearly heading downtown for the event. The bus was stopped for several minutes. I got out to see what the trouble was. One of the Peronist organizers had asked Mary to switch buses. She refused, as she has been assigned to bus number 15.

During the series of rallies, Villa Olimpia was like an orchestra without a conductor, to use the image of the French sociologist Pierre Bourdieu. It would be mistaken to position Salcedo as the conductor of these collective processes, because he was part of the political exchanges just like the rest of the neighborhood's inhabitants. His career depended on the alliance with members of the government. As a result, he was obliged to mobilize the neighborhood residents as a sign of his strength. This, however, was something that did not depend entirely on him.

The rallies depended on the supply and demand for political support, creating two categories: getting others to come and being seen. In the days leading up to each event, the members of the political group and their leader would invite the Villa Olimpia residents to come with them, visiting them at home or taking advantage of brief conversations as they walked through the neighborhood. Those who were "invited" to attend knew that eventually something might be in it for them. This is why Mary thought it was important for Liliana to attend this rally. If she wanted that broken pipe to get fixed, she had to be seen. Mary's political work consisted in reinforcing this imperative among the settlement's residents. "Once they [i.e., the network members] know you, they ask, 'Why didn't so-and-so come?'" Mary explained as she walked through the neighborhood inviting people to a new rally.

In one of these journeys, we met a resident who had stopped going to the marches after falling ill. Her health had worsened, and she was probably not up to the bus ride. Mary had prudently spoken to Salcedo about this woman's situation. When Mary spotted her, she told her not to worry, that she would receive all the medicine she needed for her recovery just the same. Before the conversation ended, Mary gave her some words of advice: "Tell your son to come to the march. That way, he can talk to Salcedo's wife. She can probably get you a sewing machine so you can get some work."

Through interventions like these, Mary reiterated her belief in the virtue of being seen, a rule of thumb that applied to most political exchanges: voicing support for Salcedo was necessary to generate an obligation for Salcedo (or his political network) to return the favor. The conviction that she helped instill in others was born from her own belief in this system. Her moral capital, which was proportional to the support she rallied around Salcedo, could be seen in how carefully Mary prepared the list of who would be on the bus for the demonstration, reminded those who had promised to go, got food and beverages for the trip, and so on. And it could also be confirmed in the number of people who attended because of her. This number was the objective indicator of both the obligations she fulfilled in the network and of those that she assumed with the settlement's residents.

Failing to Fulfill Obligations

Mary used the expression "working for Salcedo" over and over again. It summarized the shifting balance of mutual obligations between Mary and Salcedo, along with her own obligations to the settlement's residents. Her position in the political realm depended on the configuration of these obligations.

When Mary decided to step down, her political work was no longer associated with Salcedo. She could either connect with another network—word of her dissatisfaction got out and Beto Ramírez expressed interest in speaking with her—or simply put things on hold. By opting out of the Children's Day festivities, she was choosing to do the latter, that is, to exclude herself from an activity that brought together the whole neighborhood. "If I don't go, everyone will be asking why," she said, clearly bothered.

An innocent conversation about a stolen gas canister revealed that Salcedo had shirked on his obligations to Mary after she had fulfilled hers during the rallies. The intensive "political work" of those months had depended on mutual promises, but apparently all her work didn't even entitle her to the gas she needed to cook meals and heat her home. "Salcedo constantly says yes but then does nothing," she complained. "After all I've done for him he owes it to me!"

Someone had stolen a gas canister from Mary.[2] When Salcedo found out, he told her not to worry, he would replace it. She waited for Salcedo—or Kuko, his right-hand man—to buy one for her or say something about getting her a new one, but neither had contacted her. "I'm not buying another one," explained Mary. "Not because I don't have the money but because they said they'd get me one."

It was one disappointment after another. A year earlier, the house with the soup kitchen where she served snacks to the children in the settlement had burned down. She was still waiting for Salcedo's approval for the reconstruction to begin. "I've got the Paraguayans here ready to start building! Meanwhile, the kids have to go to the church for their snack."

During our conversation, she got a call from one of Salcedo's nieces to ask her about how much milk and chocolate powder was needed to feed a thousand boys and girls. "I'll get back to you," she said. It was a stark contrast from the old Mary, who used to drop everything to respond to people from Salcedo's network. Our conversation continued.

"I told Tamara she had to go to the demonstrations so that Salcedo would keep her in mind . . . And she went but Salcedo didn't do anything for her! Do you think I should go talk to Beto Ramírez? If I work for Salcedo . . ."

She didn't give me time to answer. Instead, she continued: "My daughter's house should already be finished. They had promised it for March. It's a joke! All of the neighboring houses are done, but not hers. I spend money out of my own pocket for the marches! I have to bring something to eat and drink for the *murga*.[3] They send me the kids who are hungry, and I have to feed them. Salcedo knows that, which is why he gives me a hundred pesos for each demonstration."

I spoke with Tamara at one of the demonstrations that Mary had requested she attend with her children. Tamara had never been to a rally before. She had to be seen—so that Salcedo would keep her in mind—because her husband had been arrested on drug-trafficking charges. He would only get a conditional release from jail if he could certify that he had a job. This was her request for Salcedo. Mary had assumed the obligation of getting her the certificate.

Mary was hurt by how weakened her authority was. She found out that Salcedo wasn't even going to be sending her provisions for Tamara and her children. How could she get Tamara the certificate she needed to get her husband out of jail? How could she guarantee it?

Mary's acknowledgment of her loss of authority also affected her family ties. How could she keep her position in the network and in the settlement if her own daughter had to wait to get her house built? How could she retain the loyalty to Salcedo of her sons, daughters, sons-in-law, and daughters-in-law if she herself was having trouble getting the wherewithall to reward them for their political support of him? She needed her relatives to ensure a minimum number of people at rallies, but she also needed their social and moral backing.

The flow of provisions had become more erratic over time. It was comprised of qualitatively differentiated objects, which acquired value when they circulated as part of political exchanges; when they did not circulate, one's involvement became questionable. This was Mary's current position. It undermined her authority and made her political work in the settlement difficult—not only did it lack a space in which to feed the children, but when provisions weren't delivered, she was the one who was blamed, not Salcedo. The promises she had made were thus questioned, as were the obligations she had assumed.

A Political Salary

In the end, a serious illness with which Mary had been diagnosed years before flared up on Children's Day, so she did not attend the celebration, albeit not for the original reason. When I saw her again, I found her very concerned about her health but more conciliatory: "Everything's fine with Salcedo," she said. "Oh, sure, I was angry, but he knows that whenever I get sick, I disappear. But he also knows that if something urgent comes up, I'm there, no matter what."

Since her health had made it difficult to keep her place selling food on the soccer field, her household economy had suffered. While she had previously remained elusive when asked about the money she received from her work in the political network, her current situation allowed her to speak a bit more freely: "Salcedo knows my situation. He tosses a little something my way."

This "little something" consisted of a monthly salary of two hundred pesos and a bonus that varied depending on the situation. "When I need a little more, he gets it for me," she said. In this case, the bonus was an indication of Salcedo's concern for Mary's health. Mary explained that this money was "like a plan" in reference to the government's welfare plans, "but not exactly." Unlike the welfare plan, the money she received was a personal payment. With this type of conditional cash transfer, the amount varied depending on her connection to Salcedo at the time.

The reasons that had made Mary consider stepping down faded away. In addition to the political salary, other transfers came from Salcedo's network. Her grandson received a scholarship for school; reconstruction began on the house for the soup kitchen; her daughter finally moved into her new house; and her youngest son had found a job with a construction co-op run by Salcedo's group.

The money circulated, which meant that Salcedo recognized that Mary had fulfilled her obligations. He asked her to speak of her work in the settlement during the affiliation campaign at meetings with the residents of other *villas miserias* in La Matanza. Salcedo had once again shown that he could trust Mary, that he knew she would be there when he needed her. She recovered her hopes and her expectations for the future: finishing construction on her house and getting her children "steady work," as she referred to the jobs at town hall. The moral capital that connected her to Salcedo and to the political network guided these hopes. Mary confessed, however, that she never looked more than a year into the future—that was the amount of time she considered it reasonable to hope.

Expectations

On Christmas Eve 2009, I called Mary to wish her and her family happy holidays. She was pleased I had called and said she had a lot of good news. First, one of her children had finally gotten "steady work." The position at town hall had come within the year-long deadline she had set for her expectations from Salcedo.

According to Marcel Mauss, "'I expect to' is the very definition of any act of a collective nature."[4] Bruno Karsenti offers this explanation of Mauss's affirmation on the nature of expectations:

> If expectation is preferable to obligation when describing the method of determination at work in the origin of law and economy, it is because it reveals the subject's willingness to accept the future as inevitable as opposed to the immediate imposition of being forced to act on the impulse of an external authority. . . . The individual "expects something" and acts accordingly, but the action she takes, the precise form of this action and the result it produces, remains suspended in a possibility that is encircled by a complex network of obligations. (Karsenti 1994, 50)

Political money inspires expectation with regards to the future. This is the place where Mary's hopes for her children are configured. In the preface to the compilation *Money and the Morality of Exchange* (1989), Maurice Bloch and Jonathan Parry suggest that the meanings that different cultures give to money depends on the length of the transactions. Short-term transactions are associated with competition and individualism; long-term transactions consolidate social ties. For Mary, *political* money represents a long-term wager to guarantee the continuity, not only of her family group, but also of the political network and the power of its leader. *Political* money thus symbolizes the fulfillment of mutual obligations; it functions as a currency in the moral account of political ties and thus of social cohesion.

Whether the instrumental nature of money in political contexts is examined by Max Weber or contemporary sociologists and political scientists, it tends to be unwavering, regardless of where it is used. In my work, its meaning depends on a hierarchy of money. In this chapter, the puzzle assembly approach allowed me to discover the piece of money that undergirds part of political life in Villa Olimpia. The stories of Analía, Beto Ramirez, and Padre Suárez—along with the rumors of political payments to loyal followers—show how money ranks higher than other means of exchange (e.g., medicine or food). In this chapter, I have shown how Villa Olimpia residents made *political* money the accounting unit to acknowledge the fulfillment of political obligations that bind leaders and their followers together in relationships of power. To put it more succinctly, this community places political money at the core of its collective life.

Recall that Viviana Zelizer (1996) identifies three monetary payments that people use to distinguish their social relations: gift, entitlement, and compensation. Which of these categories covers the meanings of *political* money? I believe that each of these payments contributes to the meaning that the agents attribute to this type of money. We can see this interpretation in the bond between Mary and Salcedo. *Political* money, on the one hand, took on the meaning of a gift. Mary emphasized how Salcedo showed his concern through money. When she was sick, the leader of the political network "tossed a little something [her] way." However, other meanings also emerged, such as entitlement ("After all I've done for him he owes it to me," Mary said) and compensation for tasks rendered (Mary kept a list of everything she did as part of her "political work"). These three aspects—gift, entitlement, and compensation—thus came into play, though not without conflict, in order to define a type of payment that no single one could cover on its own.

When these circulations are described by those involved in such exchanges, they are generally characterized as a gift or compensation, which indicates how this money is linked to personal debt or exploitation. Another way to interpret the connection between Mary and Salcedo is within a perspective that attempts to capture cycles of shared obligations, thus eluding this one-dimensional viewpoint. By introducing the concept of time, a uniform approach to obligations is abandoned in order to consider the way in which agents act differently depending on the point in the cycle. This way, entitlement and compensation become possible meanings of the political payment when Salcedo's favor appears further off in time. The autonomy that Mary displayed during these periods was as real and important as her acquiescence when Salcedo "tossed something [her] way" to help her get through tough times.

According to this argument, *political* money is a combination of three types of payments. No single one provides a comprehensive understanding of the meaning of money in the realm of politics. If the perspective of instrumental money comprises only one side of these heterogeneous meanings (a side in which the request for money can be considered selfish, fair, or imperative), it is because this perspective cannot capture the struggle to accumulate moral capital that is indispensable to *political* money. The positivity of this puzzle piece can thus be found in the efforts, down in the trenches where political ties are put to the test, to have one's virtues acknowledged and to reveal the other's defects.

As we have seen in the preceding pages, Luis Salcedo and Father Suárez competed for the hegemonic leadership of Villa Olimpia, and their political rivalry was rooted in a hierarchy of money. The next chapter will provide more insight into the role of the moral dimension of money in forging power relations between a leader and his followers, and the way it helps create social orders.

Sacrificed Money 5

VILLA OLIMPIA'S STORY can be told through the parish priests who have served in the parish church, which began as a chapel. The priest at the helm during my fieldwork was Father Francisco Suárez, whose family, all Paraguayan immigrants, lived in this *villa miseria*. He thus bore the stigma of being a *villero*—and suffered under the last military dictatorship's policy of eradicating the slums by expelling the inhabitants of *villas miserias* from the city of Buenos Aires.[1]

After being ordained as a priest and serving in different parish churches across the country, Suárez was sent back to the Villa Olimpia parish church in 1996. The local residents were thrilled; after all, this was a priest who had grown up in the neighborhood, someone they had known since he was a boy. The local church played a crucial role in collective life in the slum and the priest in charge did as well. Unlike other clergymen, Suárez didn't have to pretend to know the codes of the poor or make a forceful adaptation to social life in the slum.

Since the 1990s, the religious world of the poor had been increasingly shifting away from Catholicism. Other religious groups, mainly Evangelists, were now vying to be the spiritual representatives of the lower classes. In response to its weakened position, the Catholic Church strove to retain its place in the life of the poor by expanding its social assistance (Forni and Gómez 2002; Woods 2009). Father Suárez's career in the church and his work were part of this reconfiguration of Catholicism.

In the twelve years since Suárez had returned to Villa Olimpia as the parish priest, his social assistance had at times exceeded his spiritual work within the church itself. When unemployment and poverty spread in the 1990s, social assistance had been the parish church's main activity. The soup kitchen, which had opened in 1992 to serve fifty children, was feeding nearly five hundred people in 2009, including children, the elderly, adult women, and even some adult men. The activities extended beyond the soup kitchen itself and included the distribution of food and medicine boxes, used clothing sales, and a celebration of Children's Day, with free toys for the children. Funerals were also organized at no cost. In summer, the children and adolescents of Villa Olimpia were treated to excursions and camping trips. While I was spending time in the neighborhood, a home and rehab center was opened for young people struggling with addiction. In addition, a new chapel was under construction.

Money was needed to finance all of these social activities organized by the church. *Donated* money was the most important piece here, with companies, civil organizations, international organizations like the U.N. Development Programme (UNDP), and state entities all contributing to fund the priest's works.

However, this piece does not entirely explain the power of Father Suárez. In this chapter, I reconstruct the hierarchy of money that forms the basis for his leadership and led him to lock horns with the local political leader, Luis Salcedo. My goal is to provide an in-depth look at power in the world of the poor and show how these dynamics are rooted in currencies that produce social orders. Towards the end of the chapter I shift the focus from the uses and circulation of money to other goods. As my fieldwork revealed, other goods besides money functioned as currencies used to measure and compare the moral capital of the two leaders.

Mirrors

"Sonia has to be my mirror," Father Suárez repeated.

Sonia was one of the coordinators at the parish church soup kitchen, a Paraguayan woman of around sixty, mother of two and grandmother of five.

Through her, it is possible to reconstruct the history of Villa Olimpia with each of the priests to whom the parish church had been entrusted.

In her house, Sonia kept a box with pictures of each of the priests. As she showed me the photographs, she remembered their religious orders and their personal backgrounds. She was one of the locals who had most supported the appointment of Suárez. After all, it would save her having to explain to the priest how to treat the poor or help him try to adapt to class differences.

In the mid-1970s, Sonia began working at the parish church from time to time. Later, her work there became regular and she embarked upon what could be called a career in church work. With each priest, she learned more about working with the poor, eventually becoming the parish coordinator in the slums and an assistant social worker within the church.

This is how Sonia began to accumulate both social and cultural capital. She spoke proudly of her friendship with priests of more well-to-do social classes and with the relatives of certain important politicians. Commendatory certificates with her name on them also gave her great satisfaction. These allowed her to feel that the church "had given her everything" and made her proud of her status in the neighborhood.

A story about the widespread use of *political* money led me to discover a new piece of the puzzle represented by the hierarchy of money in this religious world of the neighborhood, *sacrificed* money. When Father Suárez spoke to Luis Salcedo to demand salaries for his people, Sonia informed him that she did not wish to be on the payroll. My initial understanding of this refusal was based on Sonia's explanation. Because of her involvement in Peronism and in existing political networks, she said, she still had some old friends in other wings of the party and thus was already getting a political salary. However, her refusal revealed a social order based on a hierarchy of money.

Javier Auyero (2001) emphasizes the personalized nature of the goods circulating within a Peronist political network by comparing it with a Catholic one:

> The Peronists strive to consistently hand out goods to its followers; the difference with the way the local Catholic Church distributes food is noteworthy.

In the case of the Church, the person in charge of the distribution explicitly dissociated him or herself from the goods given to those in need. The Caritas representative explains that "We have to make our collaborators understand that what we hand out doesn't belong to us . . . we are only here to lend a hand." My purpose here is not to idealize church charity, but merely mark the difference between church volunteers and political mediators. (Auyero 2001)

Laura Zapata (2005) criticizes this argument. Advancing a concept of charity that conditions the disposal of free goods, she notes that it is essential to explain why Caritas practices this dissociation, as opposed to Peronists who hand out goods and charity for their own advantage. Unlike these perspectives, which treat the world of politics and religion as two separate spheres, I propose to examine what unites these two social universes. Is it possible that the differences between them arise precisely from what they have in common?

Both religious and political networks create social distinctions among their members, but these distinctions originate from different sources, that is, spiritual power and temporal power. This interpretation is inspired by the concept of the "field of power," juxtaposing the temporal and spiritual realms, that is postulated by Pierre Bourdieu (1979), the former being identified with institutional or material reproduction, while the latter claims to transcend temporal interests. In Bourdieu's analysis, the structural constant that makes these powers collide allows this "field" to be used as a tool that helps describe hidden associations.

The identity, appeal, and aspirations associated with a given network depend on how these features are constructed in relation to their source of power. Once again, when these social universes are approached as isolated entities, there is a risk of an essentialist interpretation. Although we may call them temporal or spiritual, we are in both cases referring to some type of power, and the identity of one type depends on its difference from other types.

In a slogan hinting at a redistribution of resources, mainly money, based on a reformulation of the community (Frederic 2004), Salcedo's group proclaimed: "A project that's changing the neighborhood." The transformation of the neighborhood depended on specialized agents entrusted with obtaining and distributing the goods necessary to sustain this (new) community identity. The urbanization process was based on the availability of government resources and a political network to distribute them. No one in the neighborhood was surprised that Salcedo's organization had a fluid relationship with these goods, a relationship that would have been impossible to hide. What is more, Salcedo's organization acquired political importance through this relationship in a configuration that favored the use of money as payment for political favors.

Spiritual Power

If the political network was associated with temporal power, the religious network represented the poles of attraction and repulsion associated with spiritual power. My field notes from October 2008 are particularly illustrative in this regard.

> Sonia and I are in the parish church kitchen. People arrive with plastic containers and leave them on the kitchen counter. There are fewer people than usual, maybe because it is so cold outside, or because the previous day, the Social Assistance Department had distributed food boxes.
>
> A little girl puts down her plastic container. Sonia tells me that she has started catechism: "We are trying to get two of the girls who come to the soup kitchen to join the classes. The people at the soup kitchen don't come to church. We're like the Opus Dei people, huh?"

Opus Dei is an ultraconservative, elitist group within the Catholic Church. How could Sonia—a woman whose most cherished memory was having met the Third World priest Carlos Mujica,[2] who had opted for a Catholicism committed to helping the poor—be comparing herself with such a group?

Sonia's ironical identification with Opus Dei refers to a distinction marked by her participation in the parish church activities. From Sonia's perspective, the spatial division soup kitchen–parish represented a social division. Those who had accessed the parish church carried the symbolic power of having left behind the stigmatized space of the soup kitchen. The offer of spiritual goods and the way in which such goods were used by the Father Suárez network created social borders, which Sonia expressed by associating herself with Opus Dei.

This also explains why Sonia refused to take the *political* money: the relationship with this type of money reveals the need to reconstruct the balance of power between pieces of money that established the hierarchy of money in which she placed herself. The hierarchies between pieces of money grant status in the social world.

Sonia's comments show that the heterogeneous social orders and money hierarchies often overlap. When Sonia refused to take the money, she constructed a sacrificial micro-rite.[3] *Sacrificed* money indicates the virtue of transcending material goods. Sonia avoids *political* money by affirming that she is part of a social order that will acknowledge her for her *sacrificed* money. By relinquishing this money, she is building her moral capital and her hierarchy within the religious group led by Father Suárez. Sonia revealed this hierarchy when she compared herself to her fellow church workers.

"Claudia's got no character," Sonia said. "The other day, I said to her, 'Claudia, we have to go see this very needy family that doesn't come in to the soup kitchen. We have to go see what's going on with them.' But she just sat there. She never said, 'Yes, let's go.' And when I say I'm going, I go right on over." Then she moved to another story to explain what she meant about Claudia. "Yesterday a man needed some sugar. I *know* he needs it. How can you let a man go without sugar? Claudia didn't give him any. She picks and chooses. I don't want to make a point by what I give or who I give it to—I give whatever there is to whoever needs it."

This attitude was what Father Suárez expected from Sonia in saying he wanted her to be his mirror. Her position within the network corresponded to that recognition: Sonia presented her self-denial as a value, one she consciously emphasized by not taking advantage of the privileges that came with her involvement in the organization. She had to identify with the situation of the person in need, and the ability to forgo material goods was an asset in this regard. Those who did not practice an economy of sacrifice were drawn into question. One of Sonia's collaborators expressed it best. "Today I give what I have, tomorrow God decides."

These competitions between pieces of money represent conflicts between sources of moral capital. While it was perfectly fine for Sonia to receive a political payment from an old friend from her days in the Peronist party, accepting *political* money in the religious group would have reduced her prestige. Sonia was not against *political* money as an abstract concept; she was against it only within the social universe whose feelings and perspectives suffused another piece of the money puzzle. Accepting that money would have meant acknowledging how the balance of power between these two pieces of money had been altered, or abandoning the distinction that the religious group provided her and jeopardizing her position in the neighborhood. It would have been like admitting that she had no strength of character.

This shows that *sacrificed* money works as a critical piece in Father Suárez's group. It operates on the logic of the prestige of the label so brilliantly analyzed by Norbert Elias in *The Court Society* (1983). Every gesture that the king made entailed prestige or scorn, revealing one's proximity or distance from royal power. The label constituted a true fetish symbol. In the religious sociality we explore, *sacrificed* money has the same value. It brought power to the members of the network and distinguished them, giving access to higher-ranking positions in the network and proximity to the priest.

Sonia and the others always introduced themselves as volunteers, making it clear that they were not being paid for their work. *Sacrificed* money imposes strict regulations. People in subaltern positions accept that this piece takes priority in the hierarchy of money in the religious sphere. Sonia would say over and over again, "We're here to serve. This is not a job." The church's collaborators incorporated this perspective and categorized their efforts as "volunteer work." They reiterated the importance of *sacrificed* money. Even women who occupied the lowest ranks were asked to behave in this manner. Although they were not paid for their work in the parish, they did obtain other goods that were considered legitimate payment methods, like the food left over from lunch.

I would like to emphasize that the use of *sacrificed* money is not exclusive to the religious world. During my work, I met a range of community leaders whose political performance was identified with this piece. "I always spend money from my own pocket," they would say to back up their own commitment to political or social welfare activities.

Using Bourdieu's conceptual tools, Daniel Gaxie has proposed understanding the disinterested acts of political militants or of the volunteers of charity organizations by associating them with specific situations. Militant universes are "officially—that is, authorized in a legitimate, public, and collective manner—disinterested" (Gaxie 2005, 164). The militants adopt a disinterested tone when they are in these situations; in contrast, outside of these situations, they express personal motives. Distrust of supposedly disinterested motives requires that they be analyzed within certain spatial and temporal limits. By examining them within the framework of official situations, researchers can show how the disinterest expressed by the agents reflects pride in their own actions. This perspective depends on another important factor. The militants publicly assert their "officially disinterested engagement," and the language and actions associated with the disinterest are thus understood as intentional and deliberate.

From my perspective, comparisons between disinterest–official situation and interest–unofficial situation run the risk of becoming naturalized. Instead, I suggest three interpretations: (1) all pieces of money bear a principle of disinterest, given that they all entail an acknowledgment of virtue; (2) this acknowledgment has no spatial or temporal limitations and is found in both official and unofficial situations; (3) disinterest does not necessarily spring from intent; instead, it should be understood as part of a social norm that people generally abide by.

What follows from this perspective has less to do with interest versus disinterest than with the hierarchies between pieces of money. In this regard, the presence of *sacrificed* money in the world of politics, or of *political* money in the world of religion, speaks of the hierarchy of money that causes tension as it establishes differences between the individuals in these spaces.

Everyone's Father

Luciana is in charge of handing out food at the parish church. In August 2008, when an elderly woman asked her for food, she went back into the pantry and came back with a package of noodles and a container of milk. "I don't need the milk," said the woman, who thanked her and then left.

"You see? She had milk left over from last time . . ." Luciana winked at me and nodded in approval. "I don't give food to just anyone. I tell some of them to come back later."

"Who has to come back later?"

"It's my job to figure out who might be taking advantage of us—or identify the young people who could go out and get themselves a job. Now that woman, how can she possibly make a living? She's too old to work. Sometimes I tell people, 'If people see you coming in here every two weeks, then I have a problem. Remember that our help has its limits and try to make the food last all month. If you come by this afternoon, we serve chocolate milk. What was your name again?'"

Luciana says that if she gave food out every time she was asked, she would run out of stock in a few hours. "At the church, with the little foodstuff we have, it's important to be intuitive, to figure out who is trying to take advantage of our generosity and who actually needs our help. If the person is ashamed to ask for it, you know there's a real need."

Need requires proof. The records of food handouts in Villa Olimpia are indicative of this. Luciana made use of these intuitive classifications that allowed her to distinguish the truly needy from those who are "trying to take advantage of our generosity." In addition to these classifications, there were objective data—an elderly woman cannot make a living—to measure the moral capital of the receivers. Luciana in fact used the term "intuitive" to refer to this practical operation of distinguishing people according to a moral criterion of need modulated by a specific value: being "ashamed" to ask. Everyone else was told to come back later, another tactic she used intuitively. Luciana's colleagues had been trained to make the same classifications. On countless occasions I heard them say, "This is a big neighborhood, but we all know each other and we know who is needy and who comes in asking just because."

The moral distinction between the "good poor" versus the "bad poor" produces a social closure (Weber 2013 [1922]) around the scarce goods and opportunities that the network has to offer. It serves as the most efficient tool for social distinction and can be approached from the perspective of moral capital. However, Luciana never spoke of the "bad poor" with Father Suárez, according to what she told me in October 2008. "Father doesn't know that we don't give to everyone. He would get mad. He's very generous and he says yes to everyone. People ask him for anything, money to travel, money to eat."

"How does he do it? Does he take from his own pocket?"

"No. He asks for loans from people at our church and then he ends up turning that loan into a donation. I try to keep some of them from asking him for money. We all tell them to try to resolve things themselves and not depend so much on Father."

The way Luciana describes the priest's generosity merits attention. If Father did "everything for everyone," that was partially because this public performance rested on Sonia's and the others' ability to limit the requests that actually reached him; the goal was to avoid forcing the priest to have to say no. If he said no, that would negatively affect his image. By "budgeting" the requests that reached Suárez, the priest's name remained associated with *sacrificed* money; in this way, his charisma and his power were further consolidated.

The regular and continuous cycle of *sacrificed* money in circulation fed the individual and collective hopes mediated by figures like that of a religious leader. The roots of his moral capital were based on the belief in his power to satisfy these expectations. The pieces of money connect these hopes with the confirmation of authority, redirecting one towards another.

In the case of Villa Olimpia, the monetization of religious life was translated into a dynamic that challenged the virtues of the community leaders. Through *sacrificed* money, belief in them was reinstated. For this reason, the religious work and charisma of Father Suárez was immersed in a monetary economy.

Multiple Pieces, a Single Coin

In a footnote to *The Gift*, Marcel Mauss argues that there are other currencies besides our own modern one. To define what qualifies as other currencies, the primordial nature of money itself—its capacity to express authority and social power—must be understood.

Mauss makes this clarification in a text from 1914, *Les origines de la notion de monnaie*, which established the intimate connection between money and authority. Money gives men power, imposing certain behaviors. Money is, in Mauss's explanation, a moral authority. This idea later appears in the institutional perspective of money as presented by Michel Aglietta and André Orléan (1982) and by Bruno Théret (2008): all money is used to express the consensus of a social totality through an objective value. In other words, money materializes the collective feelings and beliefs on what holds value, maintaining a united and cohesive totality. *Political* and *sacrificed* money reveal their potential—and also their limitations—to produce this effect.

As they circulate, *political* and *sacrificed* money carry a series of social orders and hierarchies of money, which often overlap. Each piece is indecipherable outside of the hierarchy of money and at the same time projects a social hierarchy. Between the two pieces, there is fiery competition for the range of objects and people involved. The widespread nature of *political* money met with resistance, because accepting it meant eclipsing the social and money hierarchy of *sacrificed* money, to return again to Aglietta and Orléan's concept. The Villa Olimpia community could not accept such money without certain conditions.

Let me emphasize that these two puzzle pieces, regulated by specific systems of feelings and perspectives, compete with one another. They reveal how social orders and hierarchies of money overlap, though not in their entirety. There is never a consensus on what has value, but an accumulation of feelings and perspectives that transcends them and overflows. There is an excess value that these pieces cannot contain.

This interpretation poses some questions. What form do currencies capable of containing this excess value take? What monetary dynamic is revealed when this form is explored? And what dynamic do these currencies adopt in the life of the poor?

The Children First

These are my field notes from August 10, 2008, the Sunday when Children's Day is celebrated:

The chapel is only half built; the walls, floors, altar and columns were still bare concrete. The roof is open on the sides, an indicator of when the money ran out and the glass windows could not be purchased. Some tattered plastic covering has been put up to keep out the wind, the rain and the cold.

Father Suárez is leading mass with two sisters who recently arrived from Paraguay. Sonia is off to one side and near the end of the mass she sets out a table with a tablecloth near the door leading into the parish storeroom. Two collaborators bring over three cardboard boxes with white bags inside. When the mass ends, Father Suárez announces, "We are raffling toys for Children's Day. Remember that we'll be hosting the celebration on the thirteenth, with a treasure hunt."

Rosa, one of the collaborators, whispers to me, "Six hundred toys! There is a raffle now, but there will be toys for all the children this afternoon. We worked all week on this. Father loves to celebrate and we enjoy doing something for the kids."

An hour later, cumbia [tropical dance music] and lively conversation can be heard from the Community Integration Center (CIC). Inside are five inflatable castles, identical to the ones put up in the parish church.

Four rows of children line up for sack races. Each row is headed by a woman from Salcedo's group. "We're really happy to be able to celebrate Children's Day like this," one of them gushes.

In the hall where we are talking, a long table is covered with yogurt drink containers and *alfajores* [cookie sandwiches]. "Did someone pass anything out to the people sitting next to the wall?" she asks. "I don't think they got anything. They should get something."

The kids run up and down the hall, get a toy, and head out a door that leads onto the CIC patio. A cameraman is waiting there, along with one of the women who asks [the children] to say something about the toy they received while looking at the camera.

When I walk off towards the main road (which happens to be paved, unlike most of the streets in the neighborhood), I see a few kids heading into the neighborhood with the toy bags that Father Suárez had handed out a little earlier.

"They're fighting over the kids!" mutters a municipal social assistant who had come to the neighborhood on this special Sunday in August.

There is no doubt that when it comes to the needy, "doing something for the kids" is fundamental to legitimizing certain aspirations. It is necessary to reflect on the hierarchy of goods that circulate towards children in terms of the role they play not so much in fulfilling a need but in legitimizing a social position.

Months later, on a hot day in October 2008, I had a conversation with Marcia and Liliana, two of the parish church collaborators. It was noon, a time when many people were coming and going in the neighborhood. I asked them about a woman who has just walked past.

"Oh, that's Salcedo's cousin," they responded in unison.

"She's a *piripipí*," added Marcia, pushing up her nose with the tip of her finger to indicate uppitiness. "She used to say hello. Now it's, 'I've never seen you before in my life.'"

Liliana nodded, chiming in, "She never does anything for anyone."

With this observation, she was establishing a contrast between herself and Salcedo's cousin, who was in a position of privilege but didn't use it to benefit anyone but herself, according to both women.

"If I had her money, I'd open a soup kitchen for the children," said Liliana.

"But you two already work in a soup kitchen."

"True, but here we work for other people. I mean a place of my own."

The women's dispute with the cousin of the local leader was mainly about her not meeting her moral obligations. The cousin's position in the neighborhood hierarchy brought with it an obligation that, according to Marcia and Liliana, she was not fulfilling. Referring to her as snobby was actually a way for Marcia and Liliana to think about what they would do in her place, what they dreamed of: starting their own soup kitchen for neighborhood children.

Bruno Théret (2008) suggests that a community is recognized through a common account and payment unit; a group forms around a quantitative way of calculating value. The goods for children served as a common currency, objectifying an important value for the community of Villa Olimpia. Thanks to this common currency, the leaders became "a kind of official, vested by society with authority," the figure Marcel Mauss uses to exemplify the power of magicians.

Collective life in a poor neighborhood like Villa Olimpia can be explored by describing other common currencies. Let's continue the search.

Inaugurations

"Today Villa Olimpia has changed—and La Matanza has changed too!" the speaker proclaimed at an event on December 4, 2008, organized to announce a series of improvements to the neighborhood.

> So many changes. We are inaugurating this boulevard and the drug rehab center. Vice-Governor Alberto Balestrini is with us, the man of La Matanza. Then there's our mayor, the monsignor, a senator for the province, and other officials whom we'll introduce later. They are all here to cut the ribbon on the newly paved Calle Tucumán. . . . Let's go, strike up the *murga*! Let's go, Villa Olimpia!

The drums and trumpets of the band of street musicians, or *murga*, played and the announcer repeated his bit. This time, he mentioned Luis Salcedo by name. Applause was heard.

> Today is a day of celebration! A newly paved street for us to walk on—and the home and center! What a happy day for the residents and friends of Villa Olimpia. Let's give a welcome to Balestrini, the man of La Matanza; our mayor, Fernando Espinoza; the senator of the province; the monsignor of San Justo; the general coordinator of slums and settlements, Luis Salcedo; the parish priest, Father Suárez; secretaries and vice-secretaries; municipal councilors; special guests. . . . Now, a round of applause for our flag!

Argentina's national anthem played over the loudspeaker. People pushed their way to the front of the stage set up on the newly paved street leading into the neighborhood. The new youth center was strategically off to one side of the stage. The soup kitchen was handing out uncooked food for people to prepare at home so that the kitchen volunteers could spend their time organizing the inauguration. Three days earlier, Sonia had asked me, "Guess what? Everyone has heard that Father Suárez's works are being inaugurated, because he's the one responsible for all this. People from Caritas are coming and so are people from Governor Scioli's office, not to mention Espinoza and Balestrini. I heard that Cristina [Kirchner] might be coming!"

Although those involved tried to mention Salcedo and thus keep him from looking bad, the celebration was clearly about the priest's work in the neighborhood. "Salcedo is committed to helping [the neighborhood], but people are going to come because they know this is the work of Father Suárez," Sonia explained. "Though they say that they're the ones doing the inaugurating." This way of explaining events associated the inauguration with the religious network, especially one of its most valued aspects—the work of the local priest.

However, the inauguration can be explained in other ways too. In terms of the difference between the parties involved, the unity of the work, and its value to the community, the ritual of the inauguration can be seen as an exemplary moment in the neighborhood's collective life. The first speaker of the day was a social psychologist working at the rehab center. She said:

> We're a Christian community that works to nourish people's faith and encourage a vocation to serve others, to help the needy. We know that there are many needs we need to fulfill: food, health, education. We live with this truth, but the real truth is discovering that your brothers and sisters need you. [pause] Today we work with youth who are suffering the agony of drug abuse, alcoholism, and other vices. Thanks to our work in our neighborhood, we have started to address this problem. What we try to do is bring these young people back to life. All of us are part of this task. We won't be successful unless we all work together.

Three other speeches highlighted the religious exchanges behind the inauguration. Fundamentally, the ambiguity of the "work" category was clarified by associating it with the name of Father Suárez. Bishop Baldomero Carlos Martini, who spoke next, offered this interpretation: "Officials, people of Villa Olimpia and visitors, it is always a pleasure to see you all together and be able to bless and inaugurate these works with the officials and especially with Father Suárez. Sensitivity is essential to create works such as these in our country." Later in his speech, he made religious references:

> Jesus, help us to fight against what is destroying our youth. May María de Luján[4] help us discover that all of us have to make this country or no one will. . . . Fill this house and this center with your presence so that the young people understand that our society takes care of them and protects them like a treasure, let us pray. . . . Bless these parish communities, bless our parish priest. Let's all say the Lord's prayer. . . . Put your hands together, not just for Villa Olimpia, but for all the neighborhoods of our beloved Matanza, which is destined to become a national milestone.

The announcer returned to the phrase "national milestone," when he called out, "La Matanza has been changing since 2000," the date when the urbanization of the settlement began.

The next to speak was Santiago, a young man who introduced himself as a "former addict": "I thank the rehab center. God bless Father Suárez. The rehab center helped me and will continue to help me. In the future, I hope to give back to those who helped me. And I hope that there will be more people like Father who open rehab centers to fight drugs."

A woman from the group Hijo, Yo Te Amo, comprised of mothers in the neighborhood whose sons are addicted to *paco*, also voiced her appreciation for the local priest when it was her turn at the microphone: "We mothers began meeting with Father Suárez to ask him for help. We thank the Lord that he sent us a guide, Father Suárez, who shares his faith every day and tells us, 'Stand up, pray for your children.' He is always with us."

By switching from the singular to plural, the next speeches shifted the value in the inauguration from the religious to the political realm and the public works, like the new pavement that the politicians were responsible for. Here Salcedo replaced Suárez; Evita Perón[5] stepped in for Jesus; housing was the focus instead of *paco*; Balestrini and Espinoza were mentioned as opposed to the monsignor. Salcedo himself said:

Most of you know I was born here in Villa Olimpia. Thirty-seven years have passed. . . . I want to remember those who made this neighborhood great. Let's give a round of applause to all those who have worked to fix the streets and to make sure we had power and running water since I was a boy. . . . A big applause for all of them! We'll never forget them. Public works make the neighborhood what it is. And that's not done by one or two people: it takes the whole neighborhood.

Salcedo said that every opinion and every suggestion counted in the urbanization. And he developed a political liturgy:

We didn't have the chance to finish school, but we know what need taught us: there is nothing better than working on behalf of a neighbor. I would tell the mayor and all the officials that I hear talking about Evita and Perón that if Evita were alive, she would be really proud of how they are representing the Peronist party. And in the neighborhoods, if Almafuerte[6] were still alive, he would tell them not to give up even when they're down. . . . Thank you!"

The applause thundered as loud as the *murga*. Now it was Mayor Espinoza's turn to speak:

The fact is, we owe this celebration to all of the residents, all of the organizations of the public good that supported us when we decided to turn Villa Olimpia into a noble neighborhood, a place with social justice, seven years ago. It will never cease to be Villa Olimpia, but today it is a neighborhood with running water, sewers, paved streets, decent housing.

. . . . Nine years ago, this started as a project, but it took a great and courageous mayor, Balestrini. . . . I congratulate the community of Villa Olimpia and most especially, Father Suárez, Luis Salcedo, the work co-ops, for the great work they are doing. To Salcedo, I say, you were right about what you said, I see that she's around us and she's with us. . . . Evita smiles again: from La Matanza, our tiny country, her teachings become a reality again: "Wherever there is a need, there is a right." Thank you! Let's enjoy the celebration and take pride in our neighborhood! Thank you, Suárez. Thank you, Salcedo. And thank you!

The staging of the exchanges was different here. There were frictions, a competition manifested in the valuable work that each speaker chose to emphasize.

The speeches of Salcedo and Mayor Espinoza placed temporal markers on the works and associated them with the figure of Eva Perón. They made reference to a mythical past in which the locals had constructed the neighborhood, connecting the start of the urbanization with the figure of Balestrini, and guaranteed continuity through the government's support.

The ritual of the inauguration expressed the esteem felt for Father Suárez and Salcedo in terms of the valuable work (or works) associated with their names. In an ethnography focused on a favela in Brasília, Antonádia Borges (2003) clarifies something important about the life of the poor. Borges argues that poor neighborhoods are in a continuous process of construction, since something is always missing that could improve their lives. For example, people in such neighborhoods spend an enormous amount of time constructing or renovating their homes, working to get the government to improve public utility networks or lobbying to get officials to make good on promises to pave the neighborhood streets. An ethnographic study of life among the poor in El Alto, Bolivia, is indicative of this trend as well. Sian Lazar (2008) shows the importance of ribbon cuttings on infrastructure works for both members of the community and its leaders. In these contexts, both authors concur that the most important collective values are the ones aimed at improving an always precarious social and urban organization.

To understand a currency, it is important to interrogate its relationship to absolute value or a social unit, according to the institutional theories of currency like those proposed by Aglietta, Orléan, and Théret. In social worlds like that of Villa Olimpia—but also in those researched by Borges and Lazar—the resources to resolve what remains unfinished serve as common currencies, giving concrete form to the transcendent values of collective life.

The work referred to in the discourses serves as a currency, just like the gifts for the kids on Children's Day. Unlike *political* or *sacrificed* money, common currencies evoke collective authority to impose a transcendent value. The community sees itself reflected in these payment methods. The ribbon cuttings celebrate this recognition. The "work" and the "public works" give concrete form to collective feelings and perspectives. The authority of a political or religious leader stems from this economy of common currencies: their obligations to the community give them their transcendent value. The work and the toys for the children show how these obligations materialize.

These pieces of the money puzzle clearly express the generic property that all currencies possess: they exercise power over men and women, even over those who appear to control the currency.

This interpretation suggests the institutional aspect of a currency, an aspect confirmed by the ethnographic data on ancient societies. In ancient societies, goods served as payment for noncommercial obligations and for barter. When a good serves to pay one's debt with the community, it expresses a value, as when goods are used to pay taxes, dowries, or bail. As a result, this good can be a currency without being a method of exchange. Max Weber had the same idea: "The chief who wishes to keep his position must be able to compensate with gifts. This is another case where currency is not a method of exchange" (Orléan 2009).

Common currencies express the unification of a shared space in which the circulation of goods represents a commitment to all the community objectives, creating the appearance of moral unity.

When a social worker got angry because she believed the politicians and parish volunteers were "fighting over" the kids, she did not stop to think that they were vying to control the collective moral capital through these goods for the children. When a woman close to Father Suárez complained that the members of Luis Salcedo's network were upstaging the ribbon cutting of the rehab center for addicts, the same rule was being applied. When frictions and the competition between goods and people came into focus at the inauguration ceremony, the struggle to show one's moral worth through common currencies was revealed.

Again, by assembling the pieces of money, a new compass of power comes into focus. In this chapter, we have seen how hierarchies of money create tension in the world of the poor, while deciphering their collective value. Groups and people express their power through pieces of money. Some seize on the values offered by all the pieces and others choose their pieces selectively, but no single piece has a single meaning. The meaning and value depend on the way the piece relates to others, making it impossible to determine the exact value of money.

In the next chapter, I explore the moral dimension of money to understand the dynamic of intra- and interfamily power.

Safeguarded Money

6

MARY AND I WALKED past the biggest house on the block. "Look at that house," Mary sighed. "The owners added new rooms to rent them out.[1] I was thinking of doing the same."

That did not appear to be an impossible dream. In fact, Mary was already renting out a room in her house to Tamara, the daughter of one of her neighbors. She wanted to take in more renters, but she wasn't sure whether all of her children would be in favor of the idea.

In Mary's household economy, where diverse pieces of money circulated, the support of each family member was critical. Her three sons and daughter gave her a hand or sometimes stepped in for her when it came time to organize a rally in the neighborhood; they also gave her advice and support when her relationship with Luis Salcedo grew tense. Similarly, her children would have to give their approval for her to *earn* money by renting rooms. Mary was particularly concerned with the attitude towards money of her youngest son, Antonio.

"He doesn't want to work. I bet he's depressed or something like that."

She noticed that Antonio was listless and gloomy and she struggled to find words for an attitude she had never expected from a son of hers. The middle son, Sebastian, was lending a hand to an older man in the neighborhood who was teaching him masonry so that he could learn a trade and earn more. "Sebastian will do any job he gets offered," she bragged. Antonio was not in tune with his brothers' get-ahead attitude.

As we can see, Mary's household economy was not free from tensions. Bourdieu's perspective is useful in this regard. His analysis questions the unilateral point of view of a single interest in the family sphere. For Bourdieu, the family is both a field and a body. On the one hand, the family universe is subject to "physical, economic and, above all, symbolic power relations (linked for example to the volume and structure of the capital possessed by each member), its struggles for conservation and reproduction of these power relations" (Bourdieu 1996, 22). On the other hand, the family becomes an integral unit through the continual creation of feelings and affections that allows for an institutional approach. According to this approach, the family becomes a united group: "To understand how the family turns from a nominal fiction into a real group whose members are united by intense affective bonds, one has to take account of all the practical and symbolic work that transforms the obligation to love into a loving disposition and tends to endow each member of the family with a 'family feeling' that generates devotion, generosity and solidarity" (Bourdieu 1996, 22).

In the previous chapters, I explored how money produces political hierarchies as it circulates. Here I present the logic that operates when money circulates in the domestic sphere. In this chapter, I explore how the social order of the family is rooted in money. I propose to understand the power relations that give shape to this family universe through the moral dimension of money. The various aspects of money help produce a hierarchy among family members (fathers and sons, husbands and wives) to determine each family's ranking in the social order of the neighborhood. This analysis reflects the theoretical outline I presented at the beginning of this book, adding Zelizer's theoretical perspective on negotiating intimacy (Zelizer 2005) to Bourdieu's approach to power.

As we have seen throughout this book, Mary's household budget was comprised of heterogeneous pieces of money like *political* money, money *earned,* and money *donated*. She managed the family finances, an arena for negotiating economic goods and social status.[2] These multiple pieces had to be organized within the set of feelings and perspectives of *safeguarded* money. This arrangement was the product of concessions and negotiations, of solidarity and conflicts. In short, it was the result of dealings that took place within economic intimacy (Zelizer 2005). In this chapter, I am interested in exploring how negotiations around *safeguarded* money define the power and status of members of a family like Mary's. This piece of the money puzzle is the one that holds the household economy together with affective bonds. While every piece bears social hierarchies and hierarchies of money, *safeguarded money* does so within the crucial social micro-order of the family unit.

Family Finances

Claudia Fonseca (2000) has analyzed situations from the perspective of female heads of households. These situations can be found in different social units, according to Fonseca, especially among the poor. Her work analyzes the complexity of "matri-focal" family structures, noting the dominance of blood ties (between mother, sons and daughters, brothers and sisters) over marriage ties. The instability of these family groups—due to changes in the quantity of family members living in the household at any time—place the mother (or mother figure) at the center. "Regardless of its demographical connotations, we could use the term 'female head of household', but if new issues rearrange the way power is distributed between men and women in the domestic sphere, are men in fact absent in the units classified as 'mother-children'? Does the mother in fact exercise power over adult children?" (Fonseca 2000). Answering these questions means reconstructing the money dynamics that form power relations in a family like Mary's.

While Mary was responsible for the household finances, her single children who lived with her were all expected to contribute. "If they are single and they're living here, they have to give me money for food. Who does the cooking? I do. Sebastian doesn't give me money anymore because now he's got a wife and children." Mary met their nutritional needs in exchange for a money transfer. However, they contributed only a small part of their incomes, while Mary's own income all went into the household.

The financial balance of the family unit depended on how the *safeguarded* money took priority over the other *pieces*. This required discipline, not a mandate from the head of the household. The hierarchy of *safeguarded* money was achieved through concessions, tensions, and savvy money strategies, such as saving. Financial management was part of the micro-politics of the household and was implemented on a daily basis. The tactics and negotiations served to preserve the *safeguarded* money that made the family an economic unit.

Mary bought her refrigerator in installments from a woman who comes to the neighborhood to sell home appliances. When Mary began explaining the payment options to me on a November afternoon in 2008, our conversation soon turned to how she made enough to get by and her sons' contribution to the household.

"Antonio is quite the wise guy. Sometimes I'm afraid he'll never grow up."

"Why's that?"

"His friends come over and then they all go out to play pool and drink beer. They're a little old for that, and granted, I'd rather have him drinking beer than doing drugs, but he still wastes his money there. One day I'm going to march in there and then he'll see. He also spends his money on clothes, on expensive tennis shoes. But he's slow when it comes to paying me."

"What does he pay you for?"

"I put away the money the boys give me. I know how much my sons make every week. And don't they know that if something happens to me, all of this is going to belong to them? The other day Pato—my oldest—said to me, 'I paid the cable bill—twenty pesos!' I paid the installments on the fridge and when the television broke, I paid to have it fixed and used up my savings. Sure, I could ask Salcedo for it, he'd give it to me, but I don't always want to ask him."

"And when they give you the money, how do you save?"

"I give the money I want to save to my daughter, the one who doesn't live here, because if I've got that money here, I'll spend it. With the merchandise I get I can wait to use the card [the government welfare card], Salcedo's money, what the boys give me. Some months are better than others, like when I sell my medicines." Mary makes some concoctions with what she calls "medicinal herbs."

The money *earned* by her children was a frequent source of arguments. When they didn't deliver, Mary would get angry, like the time she had to yell at them to get them to work on a rainy day.

"I've reached my limit!" she shouted in Guaraní.

They had to understand how important it was to earn money. The household finances were precarious. Starting that day, they agreed on a fixed amount of fifty pesos per week each.

Had Mary's sons not responded to her demands, she might have been forced to ask the leader of the political network for more money. Since Mary preferred not to depend on the feelings and perspectives associated with *political* money, she instead pressured her children as permitted within *safeguarded* money. In addition, getting her sons to work was part of helping them assume their responsibilities as men: "Until they get married, they have to give me their money."

When her sons didn't pay, the tension in the household grew. When Mary called her youngest son immature, she did so from the perspective of *safeguarded* money. The speed with which money was spent was a factor in her negative assessment of Pato, who wasted money going out with friends but was slow to hand over what he owed his mother. This temporal difference (quick to spend, slow to pay) revealed a lack of responsibility. Mary had to stay on her toes, remind him and even pressure him to hand over a percentage of his earnings. This tension increased when Pato reminded her that he had spent twenty pesos on the cable bill or when he tried to argue against giving her a portion of money *earned* doing an odd job for a neighbor. Mary also oversaw the money her children spent on other things. Her children made good "investments" when they used the money *earned* to buy shoes or clothing, unless of course they opted to buy expensive brand items.

When it reached Mary's hands, the money *earned* by her children was transformed into *safeguarded* money in a very specific form, namely, savings. In his study of the poor, Alexandre Roig (2009) emphasizes that not only are the poor capable of saving money, they place high value on savings. Excluded from formal savings institutions in their daily economic life, the most common way to *safeguard* money involves setting it aside, a practice that is part of the set of feelings and perspectives of *safeguarded* money.[3] Saving is a monetary practice that reveals the intensity of this type.

The money *earned* by her children became savings when she took it to her daughter's house. This money was a rainy-day fund, for instance, if a home appliance needed to be repaired or a new one purchased. Through money *safeguarded* through savings, the sons' commitments and responsibilities in household finances were objectified and quantified. These savings thus indicated Mary's power over her children, while revealing how *safeguarded* money ranked higher than other pieces on the household hierarchy of money.

A Family United (by Money)

One afternoon in September 2008, Pato made a rare appearance at Mary's house. He hadn't worked for several days because of a strike at the meat-packing factory.

"You've put on a little weight," I said.

"Yes, all he does is eat," Mary interjected.

We made a few jokes about it, but I noticed that neither of them found it very funny. Extra weight was a sign of not working.

"When I'm working, the pounds come right off," said Pato. Mary nodded.

Pato went out to see about getting an odd job, taking down a circus tent near the neighborhood. When he came back, he did the math. The job paid five pesos an hour and he would work between twelve and fourteen hours a day for three days, making around two hundred pesos. He considered this good pay, and he decided to try to convince his brother Antonio to join him. Mary was proud of her son's attitude:

"Nothing puts off Pato. He's always willing to work."

The question of physical health arose yet again in our discussion, though the focus was on her eldest son's excess weight, not Mary's own sick body. I tried to give him some advice: "You have to watch what you eat and not drink too much alcohol."

His younger brothers laughed at my advice. It was hard for them to imagine Pato sticking to a diet or not drinking alcohol. He had developed a beer belly, and his family knew why. He gained weight every time he was out of work, and the laughter at it was part of this family money drama.

Following my unsolicited advice, Mary launched into a lengthy monologue that touched on the family economy and Pato's personal life:

"Pato drinks like a fish. If he gets paid two hundred pesos on a Friday, he doesn't come home until Monday, drunk and broke. If he had looked after his money, he wouldn't be in the state he's in. When he was earning a good salary—living here with his wife and kids—I said to him, watch your money, save some money. But his wife got fed up with him disappearing for days at a time and told him she was done. And she's right. He says I'm on her side, but that's not it—I just don't approve of what he's doing."

In *The Elementary Forms of the Religious Life* (1912), Émile Durkheim shows how the group imposes signs of collective belonging onto the body of the individual. For example, Australian aborigines tattoo themselves with the images of sacred beings to express their adherence to the group's collective values. The situation of Mary's son was different, as his excess weight established a distance from the family's values.

Pato's excess weight symbolized his irresponsible use of money *earned*. For Mary, it was simple and painful: when Pato had had money, he had not looked after it: "He never saved." By saving, he would have set aside money for child support and preserved the family unit. His inability to transform one type of money (money *earned*) into another (*safeguarded* money) had distanced Pato from his wife and children, and his body was a living indicator of this. Now he had to find a way to put things back together.

When Mary took sides with Pato's wife after the couple split up, Pato felt that his mother was betraying him. However, Mary also considered it fair to help him with money *lent*. "I feel bad for the kids," she would say, referring to her grandchildren. This piece circulated to make up for Pato's inability to adhere to the set of feelings and perspectives associated with *safeguarded* money. By helping her son, Mary reasserted her position as the protector of the family unit and reaffirmed her ethical stance. With this monetary assistance, she was supporting her grandchildren and assisting her son.

Mary demanded that her younger sons go out and find work whenever she ran out of money, and she *lent* money to Pato. Both were part of the same economic socialization. The money *lent* to the eldest son was an attempt to salvage his masculine moral capital (based on the obligation to take care of one's family), while the youngest sons had to give their mother money to prepare them for the day when their own masculine honor would come into play, that is, when they had wives of their own.

Mary's responsibility for supporting her children framed her relationship to money. She managed her earnings based on feelings and perspectives associated with *safeguarded* money, treating all her income as mutual (see Florence Weber 2005). This was the source of her moral capital in the family unit. Her children, however, could use the money they *earned* to purchase tennis shoes or alcohol, or use it for other things outside the realm of the household. When her eldest son spent money this way, Mary helped him out with *lent* money.

By reconstructing these money dynamics, we see how power, gender relations, and solidarity are articulated to produce the social order of the family.

Bumpy Continuity

One of the monetary resources Mary considered in her household budget was *political* money. The link between *pieces* of money allows us to assess the connections between the household and the political realm. For Mary, the transformation of *political* money into *safeguarded* money was one of her gender obligations within both her family and her political group. This meant that the money that circulated as a political salary sustained her hopes for her children's well-being, establishing her role as a mother who guaranteed the financial security of her household. That is why Salcedo's unfulfilled promises related to her household caused her more disappointment than the others. For the same reason, being low on the list of the leader's priorities was closely connected to her expectations of social continuity.

In Mary's relationship with her children, the transformation of *political* money into *safeguarded* money did not alter the family's social order through its gender status; on the contrary, it perpetuated the family order. Yet not all families were in the same position; for many, this continuity was unsuccessful.

I met Ricardo, a fifty-year-old man, in my first visit to Villa Olimpia. After serving in Argentina's border patrol, he had owned his own auto repair shop. For the past three years, he had been living in one of the neighborhood's new houses. In addition to his second wife, Paula, his youngest son, nineteen-year-old Pepe, also lived with him. His elder son, who was twenty-one, lived with his girlfriend and daughter in his mother-in-law's house, which was also in the neighborhood.

Ricardo had invited me to lunch, but I was going to have to leave early; I had been invited to accompany some of the neighborhood residents going to hear President Cristina Kirchner speak. A few miles from the neighborhood, a sewage network was being inaugurated; the ceremony was overshadowed by the executive branch's conflict with farmers in the countryside.[4] For the political leaders of Villa Olimpia, it was a critical moment to stand by the president.

As we ate, the noise of the drums mixed with our conversation. The drumming was a way to encourage the residents to come out for the rally. As the departure time neared, the drums grew louder and louder. With this noise in the background, Ricardo reflected on his involvement with politics.

"I don't get involved unless they're protesting things associated with the neighborhood. Important stuff."

He provided details during lunch to support his argument. Yet when I stood up, apologizing for having to leave early to catch the bus to the rally, Ricardo grabbed his jacket and said, "I'll come with you." He had also stood with Salcedo's group at rallies organized by the government. Suddenly his story had changed: "You know why I'm coming along? For the same reasons you are—to see what's going on."

At all times, Ricardo attempted to distance himself from politicians and from the way they employed resources such as money. His discursive performance—not attending rallies, criticizing Salcedo's group for not really working for the neighborhoods, pointing out unfinished or badly constructed houses, criticizing under-the-table agreements for new housing projects—was consistent whenever he was with me. However, although Ricardo distanced himself from the neighborhood politics in his discourse, he put in an appearance at and participated in almost all political demonstrations he was asked to attend.

It then occurred to me that Ricardo's ambiguous stance on the rallies and the protests revealed the nature of political ties within the neighborhood. Although discursively Ricardo established a distance from the set of opinions and feelings associated with *political* money, his participation indicated that he in fact upheld the principles associated with this piece of money. The moral capital associated with *political* money meant being acknowledged for participating in rallies and other activities to support the leader. Accepting the invitations and attending the rallies and marches to show his loyalty towards Salcedo were sources of moral capital in politics.

One interesting point of this ambiguity was the way in which Ricardo and one of his sons tried to position themselves with respect to money that circulated from the political network. His youngest son, Pepe, was a musician in the neighborhood *murga*, and he joined in some of the discussions I had with Ricardo in August 2008. He told me that he had been promised AR$150 for each member of the band.

"But they didn't follow through. And on top of it, they gave other people work."

He believed he was more entitled to the money. After all, he had gone to all the marches. He had been there. "Pepe is really irked at Salcedo," Ricardo clarified. "He says he's going to talk to him tonight. Salcedo promised him a job in construction working on neighborhood housing—a job for him and all the boys who play in the *murga*."

For the first time, Ricardo was revealing a curiosity similar to my own as a justification for going to the rallies and demonstrations. To let Pepe know that he believed his son had been wrong to trust Salcedo, Ricardo listed his own many failed requests for work. "I never got a thing from him," he said, adding that it was because of his involvement in the parish.

Pepe pointed out Salcedo's house. "That's where it all starts. He's playing the boys in the *murga* for fools. All of us have families and we're willing to work for the money, not just take kickbacks. We play in the neighborhood all the time. It takes a lot of practicing."

"If you see it's not working out there, you have to find a way out and look for something else," Ricardo advised.

"But if I quit, this guy'll forget all about me."

Ricardo turns to me. "I told him this year to start trade school; that way he learns something and maybe gets a job."

For Pepe, it was hard to get used to the idea of getting a job that would provide him with a salary outside the Villa Olimpia political network. Ricardo was trying to convince him of a more legitimate way of earning a living: going back to school and learning a trade.

Whereas Mary perceived *political* money as part of a strategy for social and symbolic continuity (no one in her family thought it bore any stigma),

Ricardo clearly hoped that his son would follow in his footsteps as a bread-winner. He wanted Pepe to go back to school so that he could become skilled in a trade, as he himself had done years earlier. He wanted to teach Pepe to seek out money in other ways, not through *political* money.

How can we categorize the efforts to instill certain moral values that allow people to establish a hierarchy among the different pieces of money? Safeguarding family—its values and status—is clearly intertwined with the hierarchies among pieces of the money puzzle. Ricardo experienced this in a very dramatic way, trying to convince his son that the monetary hierarchy he was aiming for was in fact impossible to sustain. The situation was particularly painful because his moral capital as the breadwinner would depend on this hierarchy. From this perspective, not all the pieces of money are equally able to become *safeguarded* money. The money *earned* through work and *political* money are at odds with each other, and their potential to become legitimate *safeguarded* money differs. This is why Ricardo harped on the value of hard work—money *earned*, in this case, ranked higher than *political* money.

Ricardo himself was unemployed. He was very depressed by the fact that he only worked an odd job here or there but was unable to find work that would allow him to earn a living. He took advantage of his handgun carry permit and his experience as a former border control officer to accompany merchants when they needed to move money; the merchants paid him in either cash or grocery store credit. He also worked at a small bookstore that he had opened at the new house he had moved into, but sales were slow. Undoubtedly, his new wife was the breadwinner.

The times in which he had owned his own auto repair shop were long gone, though the memories lingered. He would draw on these memories when speaking to Pepe about his future and giving him advice about what to do. However, the fact of the matter was that Ricardo was inadvertently legitimizing *political* money in his discussions with his son. All his talk about Pepe returning to school ran up against Pepe's anxious need to earn a living; his father overlooked Pepe's feeling of having been let down by Salcedo after showing up for so many events.

The contradiction was even more palpable when Ricardo explained how he was never considered because he belonged to the parish. Pepe rolled his eyes; he had clearly heard this many times before. Those not involved with the religious group, which competed with the political network to some degree, were much more likely to receive the benefits the political network offered. This was the case with Pepe, who considered that Salcedo's house was "where it all starts." His belief was inadvertently fostered by his father, who in his own way tried unsuccessfully to get to the leader.

Pepe continued to attend the rallies with the *murga,* and Ricardo couldn't help but hope that something good would come of it. In the end, Pepe got a job through Salcedo.

The Neighborhood Elite

In Villa Olimpia, the urbanization process revealed the objective and subjective conditions associated with social mobility. Moving upwards required economic and social capital that would allow someone to cope with the expenses involved in a new house, including extras like a nicer kitchen or living-room furniture, or a home renovation. The phrase that best summarized this process came from one of Salcedo's relatives, who was entrusted with moving people into the new homes: "People aren't really aware of how poor they are until they have to move. That's when they become conscious of everything they're missing."

This reflection isn't far from Bourdieu's conclusion on the process of reaccommodating peasants in urban apartments. "It requires a cultural metamorphosis that not all those reaccommodated are capable of, because they don't have the economic means or the dispositions to make up for this lack of means" (Bourdieu 1977). The move revealed that families were not equally able to adapt to the new reality.

Elba was a woman whose husband had left her years earlier. At that point in time, she didn't have a job and was only able to feed her children thanks to the help she received from the parish. She was the head of a family that was at a clear disadvantage when it came time to move. After a year in the new house, she did not yet feel it was her own. She couldn't afford her electric bill. She also couldn't afford to fix the door, which was about to come off its hinges, while her children came in and out of the house, leaving her sick with worry that there would be an accident. She was lacking the economic prerequisites of home ownership, which had led her to consider giving back the house. "These houses are for people who have a job or a husband who takes care of them," she said categorically.

Liliana, also separated from her husband, did odd jobs like cleaning houses and was on welfare. Less than a year after moving into her new home, a sewage pipe in her bathroom had burst (see chapter 4). Enveloped in the nauseating stench that permeated her new house, she remembered her hopes back when she had moved in: "We all wanted a nice house. Even now, that's still my dream." The problems with her new home made this merely an illusion, however, like new furniture.

Elba and Liliana were at a disadvantage when it came time to enjoying their new homes. They were both female heads of household with unsteady incomes. On the opposite end of the spectrum were the families that successfully occupied their new homes at the material and symbolic levels.

These families—the successful ones—wanted to show me each room in their new homes; there was pride in this guided tour, which included the story of their move and their projects for expanding or renovating the home. After living in a space where the houses ran together along narrow corridors, the inhabitants of the new homes wanted to put up walls to divide the lots, and some constructed walls higher than the maximum permitted by the state-sponsored programs. Many waited for a family celebration to inaugurate the house; by synchronizing the housewarming with a birthday or anniversary, they marked a new stage of their lives. They experienced this as an opportunity to shake off the stigma of being a *villero*, of no longer being seen as immoral or illegal (Guber 1984).

A merchant whose two children attended a private school in downtown San Justo emphasized one change since her move to a new house two years earlier. "When we were in the slum, my children could never invite friends over. Now they can! Because they have a home just like their classmates. And to top it off, the other mothers ask, 'What did you do to get a house this nice?'"

As we can see, some families get stuck when attempting the material and symbolic appropriation of a new home. Yet for the others, the ones who successfully met the challenge, one piece of money was particularly important: money *safeguarded*, the money they had saved. In the subjective and economic adaptation to the new home, the feelings and perspectives associated with this piece of money organized the household economy, creating a collective strategy for seizing on opportunities of social mobility.

Safeguarding money through savings was a form of social continuity, a way to improve their living conditions. The importance of this piece of money reveals that each family approaches its social and symbolic continuity in different ways: the set of feelings and perspectives associated with money *safeguarded* was also distributed unevenly because not all of the families were in an equal position to save money. Below I explore this interpretation and its consequences for the hierarchies among Villa Olimpia families through a specific practice for saving money: rotating credit groups.

The Money Circle

Rotating credit groups (*círculos*, *ROSCAs*, *tandas*, *tontines*) are one of the systems of informal credit among the poor that have received the most attention from scholars (Geertz 1962; Lomnitz 1975; Singerman 1995; Biggart 2001). Members of a ROSCA, usually numbering ten to thirty, come together monthly or weekly to make a contribution to a common fund, which is lent in turn to each member until all members have been paid out.

Juana was a member of a savings circle, along with twelve other people. Each of them chipped in AR$200 a month and received AR$2,400 once a year. Juana had used the funds to pay for her daughter's fifteenth birthday party.[5] Among her myriad experiences in credit groups, Juana had invested money in her grocery store in Villa Olimpia, renovating and stocking it. The last time I saw her, she was a member of two different credit groups. Each of them had a different system, a different number of members, and varying monthly amounts.

One of the credit groups had twelve members, all neighbors and relatives, who each paid AR$100 per month and got back AR$2000. Another Villa Olimpia resident who participated in this circle, Mirta, wanted to use her payment to buy an awning for her store so that customers would come even if it rained. There were twenty people in the other circle she was in, each contributing AR$50 per week. "These are credit groups for smaller things," Mirta explained; they involved smaller amounts of money but the turnaround was quicker. While the money saved in the monthly circle was classified as an investment, the weekly contribution was for immediate or urgent situations. "When you have kids, it's good to have some money saved," she explained. For example, she had financed her daughter's birthday party through a savings circle she had participated in for a year and a half.

Mirta's sister, Silvia, was planning to join a different circle to save some money. Silvia wanted to buy dollars in anticipation of an upcoming move.[6] In a circle she was already participating in, ten people contributed AR$100 every month; in the circle she planned to join, members would contribute AR$400 per month for seven months and each member would receive two payments of AR$1,400.

For Silvia, the money from the credit groups had a clear purpose: "It's for buying big things, like paying for a new television in cash." This is how she had purchased her washing machine and refrigerator. Her niece Clara had planned to pay for her own daughter's fifteenth birthday party with money she'd saved in the previous circle, but she was forced in the end to use it to pay for her father-in-law's funeral.

Jane Guyer (2004) characterizes the poor economies of Africa as "cash economies," since the advantages or disadvantages of transactions are closely linked to access to cash. Informal savings groups are strategies to better position oneself within a cash economy. Mirta thinks so as well. "It makes a real difference when you have cash in hand," she says, before sharing a personal experience. "It happened to us: that window would have cost us four hundred and fifty pesos in installments but we got it for three hundred. That's a difference for us—we don't pay interest. It's a benefit for poor people like us; for rich people, five hundred or a thousand pesos make no difference, but it makes a difference to us. Poor people deal in cash."

Relying on stable social ties (family ties, neighbors, or friendship), informal savings groups created spaces for economic socialization. This monetary practice was unequally distributed according to one's payment capacity, and generally everyone knew who was earning enough to pay the periodic installments. Other considerations besides financial stability were critical to the success of this money practice.

The process of building the circle involved three moments when the evaluation of a member's moral capital was decisive. The first was determining who met the prerequisites to form a circle; the second was deciding whether a potential member had the prerequisites for joining, and the third was evaluating how the circle members would spend the money once they got it.

The person who started a circle was the first one who had to prove his or her economic and moral worthiness. On the other hand, the circle produced a social enclosure using moral assessment criteria. The virtues that were emphasized were like a right of entry. The *safeguarded* money of the organization could not circulate unless members of the group were recognized as having these virtues. All of them had to be honest, responsible, and trustworthy.

"If you don't have a job but we know you are hard-working—that you're out of work not because you're not willing to work but because something happened to you, like an accident, then we'll support you," Mirta explained. "Maybe you find someone who lends you your part and then you pay them back. . . . The money has to be there. We know everyone's situation."

For the very same reason, people could dig their own graves. "Since everyone knows everyone here, if someone doesn't chip in their share, we blacklist them. My brother-in-law invited us to join a circle that cost two hundred pesos per month. We couldn't join because that was a lot of money. So I told him, 'Tell me who they are and I'll tell you whether or not they're swindlers.' And I found out about one of them. 'Steer clear,' I told him, 'because one of the guys had had a problem in another circle. Watch out for yourself, because I know you're responsible.'"

Even if she had had AR$200, Mirta would have passed on that circle, because her assessment of the participants was a critical part of the decision to join: she already knew that one of the circle members had not fulfilled his obligations to another group of the same sort.

When Mirta mentioned that you got to know people better in the credit groups, she pointed out how close ties could be put to the test through the circulation of money. Blacklisting a person who didn't fulfill his obligations in one of the credit groups showed how personal relationships could be ruined as a result. For this reason, the circle exerted control over its participants by linking *safeguarded* money with affective bonds.

Sustaining moral capital inside a circle means running a tight ship at home. It is worth analyzing how the circles generate the feelings and perspectives of *safeguarded* money and the discipline imposed on the people and families who participate in them. In September 2008, Mirta described her entry into this system in terms some would use for being born again into religion:

"If I keep that money, I spend it. The circle brings responsibility. You say, 'I spend a hundred pesos a week,' but when you've got twenty-four hundred pesos, it's not the same," she says, noting the responsibility such an amount implied. "When you've got cash on hand, you spend it. That used to happen to me. I wasted my whole salary on gifts. I love giving. . . . Now that money goes to the circle. Chipping in your share each week is a big responsibility. There were a few weeks when I didn't have very much, and it was hard to get the money together. . . . But what could I do? I had to get the money somehow."

For this reason, seasoned circle members insisted on paying by the stipulated deadline and never falling into debt. "No matter what happens, even if someone dies. . . . It doesn't matter: you have to chip in, as if you were buying something. You chipped in for me, I'm chipping in for you," Mirta said. This conviction implied that the money *safeguarded* in the circle ranked high in the hierarchy of money of the household budget. "We know that when our husbands get paid, a hundred pesos automatically go into the circle. Even if you've lost your job, you have to get that money. If someone doesn't pay, they're blacklisted," adds Mirta.

The risk of abandoning the set of feelings and perspectives of *safeguarded* money that is respected within the circle could affect one's family status. Maintaining this piece in its hierarchical position protects one's social rank. *Safeguarded* money once again highlights the way social hierarchies overlap with hierarchies of money: if you have a certain status, you don't want to lose it. In fact, making a conscientious effort to *safeguard* money is tantamount to seeking a prestigious social position in the neighborhood. The circle had its own procedures for testing those whose moral capital was already in the red.

"If you don't trust someone, you put them last on the list. If you give [the money] to them at the beginning, you might get screwed later. We told one boy, 'If you want in, we'll put you last on the list, and you can rebuild your credit, you can change.' And now he's working hard—he wants to make things right. By accepting the last spot, he is setting an example as someone who fulfills his responsibilities," Mirta explained.

Time serves as a gauge and a test, though the individuals already recognized for their moral capital do not need to prove anything. "Maybe someone just moved and they need to buy something . . . or there's a birthday. . . . Everyone tells the others what they need," Mirta said, describing the collective oversight of how the circle's money was used. "We all find out what they're using the money for. We all know each other here." Mirta recalled one case with a negative outcome: "Some neighbors said they needed the money to make a trip to visit a sick relative, but then they used it to go on vacation. We found out and asked them, 'Why did you lie to us?' They were too ashamed to admit the money was for a vacation."

Using the circle's money for vacation was seen as wasteful, thus placing that participant at a disadvantage within the circle. The need to (ap)prove the use of the money lies at the center of the feelings and perspectives of safeguarded money in the circle. Certain uses were considered more legitimate than others, creating a hierarchy in the access to the money. In other words, *safeguarded* money implied moral consumption. Mirta was emphatic that credit group funds should never be used to purchase anything illegal or in her opinion to buy expensive tennis shoes.

"Spending three hundred pesos on tennis shoes is the *villero* mentality. In the circle I'm in, we don't use money for things like that. I wouldn't like it to be for that." Her participation in the circle was associated with legitimate uses for savings, like home renovations or the purchase of a home appliance, as distinguished from unproductive *villero* expenditure (Figueiro 2013). As we can see, participating in a credit group is about much more than saving for a special occasion. For its members, it means being part of a hierarchy of money that makes them part of a social group with lofty moral values.

A Future Filled with Hope

The dynamic of feelings and beliefs associated with money *safeguarded* in the circle organized the *pieces* in household budgets into a hierarchy, establishing legitimate uses for savings and demonstrating one's moral capital. When new contexts for the social and symbolic continuity of families arose, some of them were able to realize their aspirations through *safeguarded* money.

The Gutiérrez family was just such a family. The eldest daughter, Florencia, who was twenty, wanted me to avoid the less desirable characters in the neighborhood and sought to introduce me to people outside the political network who were not involved in the illicit economy. She wanted me to leave with a different, more positive image of the neighborhood. "I'm going to introduce you to the neighborhood's future social worker," Sonia said, and she introduced me to Florencia, who told me about the activities she was involved in, along with other young people, in the parish. A few weeks later, I met Florencia's mother, Juana, one of Father Suárez's assistants. Juana worked at a private school in exchange for free tuition for her younger children, without receiving a salary. She also sold beauty products in the neighborhood to supplement her husband's income. Her husband worked for a company that sold its products at supermarkets, and on Saturdays he delivered bottled soda water.

The money from the credit groups was crucial to the Gutiérrez family moving into their new house. "The credit groups have helped us a lot. They allowed me to finish up some things at home," Juana told me. When they moved into their new house, they had added a bathroom and shelves in the kitchen. When they wanted to add a cabinet under the sink, they financed the installation through a circle.

Whenever I spoke with Juana, she emphasized that her family was different from many others in the neighborhood. "They aren't like those kids who use *paco*," she emphasized when speaking of her children. And in case I had any doubts as to her ranking in the neighborhood hierarchy, she added, "You know what? The other day, my son told me that we are not living below the poverty line, because more than one member of our family works. I laughed and told him we should send Fabricio [her youngest son, aged ten] out to find a job, and then we wouldn't even be poor anymore."

Based on the statistical concept of the poverty line, the family was thus able to confirm its perception of itself as different from the others in the neighborhood. To sustain this view of themselves, it was necessary to increase the family workforce, organizing the household budget through *safeguarded* money, and using the money to ensure that the children would get ahead in life.

To return to Florencia, it was no coincidence that Sonia introduced her as "the neighborhood's future social worker." The moral values associated with this choice were the same ones valued in money circles. By safeguarding money, the family expressed its social aspirations; the young woman's decision to work towards a prestigious degree (nursing and social work were both highly respected fields) manifested the intergenerational transmission of these values. The *safeguarded* money made a material and symbolic contribution to distinguishing the Gutiérrez family in the social order of Villa Olimpia.

This chapter seeks to show how the social order of the family (the status and authority of its members) is rooted in a hierarchy of money. Taking Viviana Zelizer's analysis a step further and employing one of Pierre Bourdieu's key concepts, it further challenges the separation between intimacy and economic relations. Bourdieu's view of the family as a field crisscrossed by power relations becomes richer when the moral dimension of money is used to understand the relations between family members.

Ranking the different money pieces and reassembling them is essential to understanding how intra and interfamily power is rooted in a money structure. The different pieces of money (with their hierarchies, tensions, and conversions) form a unit that allows us to observe and understand the family universe. On the one hand, they help us understand intergenerational relations. I argue that parents instill an understanding of the value of *safeguarded* money into their children. This piece of money shows how people create and recreate the family social order in the sphere of money, which involves both mutual assistance and conflicts, helping complete family projects or tearing them apart. On the other hand, they help us understand gender relations as well. *Safeguarded* money provides a piece of evidence that applies to all the *pieces*. Its circulation carries gendered obligations; men and women are judged based on whether they meet these obligations. Poor women are viewed positively when they *safeguard* their households both emotionally and economically. In the hands of women—as we saw in the case of Mary, but also in the case of the other women who participated in credit groups—money had to be used to guarantee family continuity. Any other use of the money would be questionable, transforming the *safeguarded* money into *suspicious* money.

Previous chapters show how money is implicated in the struggle for power among neighborhood leaders. In this chapter I show that the moral capital of families also revolves around money. Using this perspective, I interpret the differences in the status and power of Villa Olimpia families. As in Norbert Elias and John Scotson's interpretation of power relations in *The Established and the Outsiders*, the members of certain family groups consider themselves superior to their neighbors based on certain money practices such as their participation in rotating credit groups. Yet unlike this classic study, which neglects to address money, in these pages I have shown the crucial role of money practices, examining how they construct moral hierarchies in Villa Olimpia, a social universe where poverty and marginalization are also the norm.

Conclusion

ACCORDING TO C. WRIGHT MILLS (2000 [1959]), knowledge is guided by an imagination that seeks connections where there apparently are none. Money, in this book, embodies this sociological imagination. Through it, we have traveled into spheres of social life that are generally analyzed separately, such as family, politics, religion, and the marketplace. Instead of providing fragments of knowledge, the aim has been to highlight the continuity among these spheres. In this book, money has served as a conceptual and methodological tool to restore connections within social life that appeared lost.

I met Mary at the beginning of 2008 during a trip to greater Buenos Aires to research the profound transformations in the living conditions of the lower classes. The initial search that led me to Mary was aimed at testing the categories most commonly used to refer to political ties, such as political clientelism. That first meeting with Mary was followed by others. My regular visits to her house in Villa Olimpia coincided with a shift in my own research interests. While I initially hoped to examine Mary's involvement in the local Peronist party, over time this fragment of her personal and collective life appeared insufficient. I gradually realized that a sociology of money could provide insight not only into the power relations at work in politics but also into those arising from other contexts and social ties. Mary was my constant guide on this journey to explore the complex forms, uses, and moral conflicts of money in the world of the poor.

In this book I have shared scenes of the daily life of the inhabitants of the poor neighborhoods of greater Buenos Aires and captured their voices. Among the many figures of this world, there are the *cartoneros* in La Matanza and the street magazine vendors, who refuse handouts because accepting them would make them appear to be part of a stigmatized social group. Luis Salcedo was another important figure in this tale, a political leader in Villa Olimpia whose followers did not necessarily view their political salary as corruption. These recipients of *political* money considered their payment to be recognition of mutual obligations and a way to measure and rank their involvement in the neighborhood's political network. Later, there was the story of Father Suárez, whose rise as the religious leader of Villa Olimpia paralleled that of Salcedo, setting off a dispute over the moral use of money in the community. Suárez's authority was based on *sacrificed* money. Marga, who liked to emphasize that the source of her earnings was her effort and dedication, was another figure in this world. Others included "El Loco" Peralta, who presented the money *earned* from selling stolen goods as legitimate income, and Cosme and Marcela, whose hard-earned reputation allowed them to continue making money from the numbers racket. We also met Juana, Silvia, and Mirta, women known in the neighborhood for saving money and thus improving the quality of their lives, and Mario, an employee at the local branch of Banco Azteca, who visited the homes of his clients to evaluate their creditworthiness and swore that the poor are more trustworthy than the well-to-do. Through these scenes and voices, this account identifies the moral dimension of money as a way to understand power relations in the world of the poor.

This world has been presented here through diverse aspects of social life, including politics, religion, culture, family, work, and the economy. From this fragmented perspective, social scientists have reconstructed the world of the poor based on overlapping models that emphasize the differences between these areas of life. In contrast with sociology's choppy representation, the lives of people like Mary reveal a continuity between the worlds of politics, religion, family, and the economy. In fact, political mediation, which researchers have used in the past to interpret the conditions of social integration, did not provide me with a unified perspective on the lives of the poor. The shift towards another area (religious mediations, for example) was equally unproductive. I encountered an enormous discrepancy between the real-life connections and the theoretical disconnections that kept researchers from providing a global view of the world of the poor.

Classic social theory helped me in the journey this book entailed. In particular, Marcel Mauss's *The Gift* served as a travel guide. In the introduction to this work, Mauss clarifies that it will lead us through time and space to places far and near and times past and present. The gift serves as a compass, faithfully pointing the way to the concrete and complete realities of different sites and moments in time. In all of these realities, the gift allows us to inquire into the connection between people. And the answer will always waver between interest and disinterest, between autonomy and subjugation. This word "integration," a concept very dear to the sociological and political tradition that influenced Mauss, takes on a different meaning when these fluctuations are incorporated.

In writing this book, I also had a compass. It was not the gift but money. Money became the vehicle that allowed me to reconnect fragments of individual and collective life. It served as a tool that could piece together the discontinued representations of the world of the poor. Without a doubt, money embodied a symbol of integration within the collective (as Simmel proposed) but taking into account the adaptations of this notion in a text like *The Gift*. In my journey, integration and power relations were not two sides of the same coin: they were both the coin.

The Theory and Method of a Moral Sociology of Money

Sociology is self-evidently more interested in the social realities that money helps to produce than in money itself. If money is morally ubiquitous, it is because it helps produce moral hierarchies and power relations. This book thus analyzes the way in which social orders founded on money come into being. This interpretation involved connecting money, morality, and power within an original analytical framework based on the concept of moral capital. This concept allowed us to see how money creates a moral hierarchy among individuals, thus producing power relations based on each person's ranking.

In my reading of Bourdieu, the French sociologist's work can contribute to the sociology of morality. In this reading, I consider the concept of moral capital as a subtype of symbolic capital. This concept contributes to strengthening the new sociology of morality by showing that morality and power are not exclusive. What is unique about this concept is the way power struggles and relations revolve around the acknowledgment of moral virtues. This concept shows that morality is not an external, universal principle of human relations but an agonistic space where these relations can be evaluated, compared, and ranked.

My argument led me to show that the concept of money developed in Pierre Bourdieu's work does not provide a detailed or complex enough perspective on the way money produces hierarchies of morality and power relations. The concept of money presented in his work reflects the approach of classical sociology, which posits that money is a tool that impersonalizes social relations. In order to refine my own approach, I combine Bourdieu's sociology of power with Viviana Zelizer's sociology of multiple monies.

This theoretical shift takes into account a new property of money: its use as a unit of moral accounting. This reveals how money can be used to morally assess and compare people. In order to capture this property, I proposed the notion of pieces of money and their hierarchies. The monetary order that results from the hierarchy among pieces of money plays a crucial role in producing moral capital. This moral capital, in turn, establishes people's status and power. My argument is based on the idea that social orders (people's status and power) are rooted in monetary orders (hierarchies between pieces of money and the social relations shaping those hierarchies).

To summarize, the theoretical shift of this book consists in moving Pierre Bourdieu's sociology of power towards a moral sociology of money and moving Viviana Zelizer's sociology of money towards a sociology of power.

A certain attitude is required for a conceptual shift of this kind. To go beyond a conception of money as a homogeneous, stable object that always produces the same effects, it is necessary to approach money as one would a puzzle. This means abandoning a holistic assumption that social life is coherent and organized. Reviewing the Spanish-language original of this book, Taylor Nelms alludes to Marilyn Strathern's observation "that there are important methodological consequences when a researcher chooses an analytical holism (as opposed to an ontological or metaphysical holism). Effectively, this perspective allows for curiosity given the fact that, according to holistic parameters, any piece of information, any act, any empirical revelation could prove relevant" (Nelms 2015, citing Strathern 1999, 7–8). The analytical holism that Nelms attributes to my work lies in assuming that the meanings of money in social life are enigmas that can only be resolved when the pieces of money are extricated, identified, and assembled. The configuration and assembly of the pieces depends on people's power and status. For this reason, the moral sociology of money depends on these assemblies to analyze the cohesion and conflicts that characterize social life.

The Power of Money Pieces

Scholars are not the only ones who have rediscovered money in the world of the poor. Development experts have created a new paradigm focused on putting money in poor people's hands, acknowledging their financial savvy, and developing institutional settings that allow low-income people to move up in the world. The moral sociology of money allows us to transcend the narratives associated with this new paradigm and the argument of its critics. Some development experts contend that access to money favors freedom and empowerment, turning those at the "bottom of the pyramid" into the new heroes of global capitalism (see, e.g., Prahalad 2005). Another narrative argues, however, that money corrodes moral ties and conveys individualistic values, serving as a means of exploitation (see, e.g., Klein 2008). These mutually contradictory narratives both treat the moral value of money unilaterally, each conceding it only one meaning and excluding any other.

My work questions these one-sided narratives of money by showing that no single piece of money possesses a single meaning. The value of each piece depends on the place it occupies in a hierarchy of money. This makes it impossible to attribute an absolute value to money and thus praise or condemn it.

Over the course of our narrative, we have analyzed face-to-face interactions on the street, witnessed sales transactions between vendors and customers, and explored the daily lives of families, political parties, and church groups. The aim of this journey was to show that the social order at work in these interactions is sustained by the hierarchy of money's different pieces. The dynamics of money (hierarchies, tensions, conversions) involve the definition and negotiation of one's status and power in specific social orders. How do street vendors handle their contacts with buyers without taking into account the difference between money *earned,* money *requested,* and money *stolen*? How could the *cartoneros* deal with the locals in Rufino unless they excluded *donated* money, which could lead them to be confused with those "living off the state"? Could Salcedo's political network hold up over time without the hierarchy provided by *political* money to gauge the dedication of each of its members? Or could Father Suárez continue to increase his sway in the slum if it weren't for the fact that *sacrificed* money ranks higher than *political* money? Would Marga keep her reputation as a trustworthy saleswoman in the neighborhood if her actions were not positioned within the hierarchy of money *earned*? We could also ask ourselves whether parents can teach their children certain values without incorporating the hierarchy of *safeguarded* money. And finally, in a context where indebtedness is a condition for accessing consumer goods, could families increase their purchasing power without the hierarchy of money *lent* establishing an ethos of responsibility in the face of debt?

The answers to these questions coincide with our findings, affirming that hierarchies among people and among different pieces of monetary are interconnected. This reveals the overlap between social orders and money orders. In our telling, the hierarchies of money are unquestionably connected to moral hierarchies.

Based on the findings of this book, a question arises: do the pieces of money build on an accepted hegemonic hierarchy? In these pages, hegemony was not as evident as the conflictive dynamics at work behind the hierarchy of the pieces and their impact on constructing a social order. One of the main contributions of this book lies in showing that social life can be analyzed through the dynamic that expresses the struggles to accumulate moral capital through hierarchies of money and to interpret how best to handle one's social relations implicated in those hierarchies.

Beyond Villa Olimpia

Each chapter of this book contributes to a better understanding of the moral sociology of money, which in turn contributes to other areas of knowledge within sociology. In chapter 1, we saw how the concept of moral capital becomes a key piece for interpreting credit relationships. Borrowers and lenders adopt different sorts of guarantees to provide certainty that money *lent* will be returned. The moral sociology of money provides insight for a sociology of credit, revealing how the evaluations and interactions between those who lend and those who borrow always take into account the virtues of the borrowers. Moral capital is ubiquitous in credit relations, be they formal or informal, inside or outside a bank.

The world of the poor is frequently depicted through stereotypes that contrast the "decent" poor with those who follow the "code of the street." On occasion, these stereotypes are even part of sociological narratives of urban poverty (Wacquant 2002). Especially in chapter 2—but throughout the book—I have challenged such depictions, showing that it is necessary to reconstruct the rules for accumulating moral capital in heterogeneous contexts. Through the concept of moral capital, each of these universes can be analyzed by identifying the struggle to have one's virtues recognized wherever one goes—in the underground economy, politics, the world of religion, or the family sphere.

Charles Tilly (1999) noted that Viviana Zelizer's sociology of money is particularly useful when criticizing a monolithic conception of state power. *The Social Meaning of Money* shows how in everyday life, people rework the standardization of money imposed by the state. The sociology of money that I present here does not present the state as monolithic or as "all-encompassing and regulative," a conception of the state criticized by John Dewey (quoted by Linhardt 2012). The moral sociology of money problematizes these representations of state power. We saw in chapter 3, for example, that the social hierarchies constructed in the lives of the poor through welfare assistance are not top-down constructions. The ethnographic reconstruction of the uses of money *donated* by the state does not reveal the imposition of a principle from another social order. The moral sociology of

money reconstructs an antagonistic space by identifying the ethical rankings that are translated into distributive criteria for the money *donated* by
the state. As I showed when analyzing the reactions to my newspaper editorial in chapter 3, money *donated* is a piece that reveals moral disputes
within the social order, the right to social protection, and the definition of
the meritocratic poor.

The moral sociology of money contributes to a better understanding
of the role of money in political life. Political ties are not insusceptible to
money: instead, money can be used to put them to the test. As we saw in
chapters 4 and 5, money can be a way to gauge people's compliance in a
political or religious network. The competition among group leaders is organized around money. Money offers a concrete measure of political commitment, pinpointing the moral value of people's actions and their political
virtues or defects. Drawing on Max Weber, it could be said that the moral
sociology of money becomes a chapter of political sociology when one ad-
mits that without money there are no politics—especially no democratic
politics—and that money elicits many feelings besides suspicion in political
life.

If the family can be analyzed as a field, following Pierre Bourdieu, then
it must also be understood through the way in which intimate relationships
affect money dealings, as Viviana Zelizer would have it. As we saw in chapter 6, the moral sociology of money puts both in perspective by moving
towards a new sociology of the family. Here the family order is yet another
realm where money helps construct power relations among family members
of different genders and different generations.

Finally, this book contributes to a novel perspective of the sociology of
morality. An absolutist perspective divides the social world between moral
actions and individuals versus immoral actions and individuals. By using
the concept of moral capital, sociology can instead show how all social universes define their own rules for acknowledging virtue. This concept thus
contributes to an understanding of the myriad sources for recognition of
moral virtues. According to this perspective, all judgments and absolute
moral assessments are relative, ensuring that no universe or individual holds
a monopoly on morality. By challenging absolute judgments through an understanding of the conditions that lead to such judgments and the effects

they produce, this program of moral sociology can contribute to a broader reflection on how society defines its conflicts, hierarchies, distributive principles, and so on.

These contributions from the moral sociology of money stem from an ethnographic reconstruction of the everyday lives of poor people who live in Villa Olimpia, Buenos Aires. In this work, I have identified and assembled the pieces of money that best captured the dynamics of solidarity and conflict that characterized social bonds. However, this book takes the arguments, concepts, and empirical evidence presented in the hope of reimagining economic sociology (Aspers and Dodd 2015) outside Villa Olimpia and the world of the poor. The moral sociology of money that I propose here is a theoretical and methodological toolbox that can be applied to other social worlds, establishing bridges with other areas of knowledge in sociology.

Georg Simmel considered that over time, money would become a global means of exchange. Like other authors, I believe that Simmel's maxim holds truer than ever in the twenty-first century. In this context, it is even more necessary to focus on how money works in social life. In this book, we have explored the roles of money that do not appear among its functions in economics textbooks. Along the way, we hit upon subjects such as hierarchy, domination, status, and competition. These themes have allowed us to reconsider the moral dimension of money as part of power relations. In short, the aim of this book was to assemble a toolbox based on the moral sociology of money to understand the role money plays in social life today.

Methodological Appendix

While this book presents the findings of different investigations I conducted between 2004 and 2009, most of my argument is based on fieldwork I conducted in Villa Olimpia and neighboring retail areas over the course of 2008 and in the last two months of 2009. Villa Olimpia is one of the many *villas miserias* in the sprawling suburbs of greater Buenos Aires.

There is no precise formula for successful fieldwork. In my experience, the most important thing is to stay alert: any conversation, interaction, or connection can unexpectedly lead us into the field. I came into contact with Villa Olimpia fortuitously, while doing boxing practice at a gym in the city of Buenos Aires. At that point, I knew I wanted to do fieldwork in a poor neighborhood on the city's outskirts, but I didn't know where. While boxing, I met M.H., who was studying to be a social worker. As we boxed, we discussed our respective work lives. When M.H. heard what I was looking for, he told me right away that the place for my study was Villa Olimpia. He had been visiting the neighborhood as the representative of a foundation that donated food to the parish church there. "You absolutely have to go to Villa Olimpia," he insisted. "So much goes on there." Had M.H. not made the suggestion, I never would have visited the neighborhood. The first lesson of this brief summary is that ethnographic work begins before reaching the fieldwork site, by keeping an open attitude and taking advantage of the unexpected.

My first meeting in Villa Olimpia was with Sonia, an active collaborator in the parish church headed by Father Suárez, whose story I tell in chapter 5. Father Suárez later joined our conversation. As an outsider, this first contact with the priest proved important during my later visits to Villa Olimpia, since my connections with him and other parish members legitimated my presence in the neighborhood. These contacts also allowed me to expand my network of contacts and reach the many informants whose stories are shared in this book.

Fieldwork can often involve uncertainty and situations that appear out of the blue, and one can never be sure of being in full control of what is happening. My experience in Villa Olimpia was no different, but establishing a routine helped keep such uncertainties to a minimum. Just as it is important to keep an open mind and be prepared for the unexpected, it is also important to organize one's daily research in order to win the trust of the people one comes into contact with, who may eventually become informants. For twelve consecutive months, I visited Villa Olimpia three or four times a week, stopping by the parish church every day. At the start of my fieldwork, this was because I had yet to establish fluid contacts with the inhabitants of Villa Olimpia and thus depended on Sonia to introduce me to new potential informants. Over time, my stops at the parish church were less about expanding my network of contacts and more of a ritual in which Sonia became the "gatekeeper" of my fieldwork. Not visiting the parish or not keeping her abreast of my fieldwork would have meant breaking the implicit agreement that had given me access to Villa Olimpia.

During the first phase of my fieldwork, my visit to Villa Olimpia required me to spend several hours in the parish church talking about what was happening in the neighborhood. These conversations with Sonia and another of Father Suárez's collaborators kept me informed about the latest in politics—like a recent visit by a government official—or any tension between the two most important leaders in Villa Olimpia: the parish priest and Luis Salcedo. Through regular visits, I was able to put together a bird's-eye view of the community, its activities, and its characters. When these same people later invited me to their houses to have lunch or share a *mate*, the locals became more aware of my movements within Villa Olimpia. Over time, I came to be known as "the boy with the parish," since I was most frequently seen at the soup kitchen organized by Father Suárez or walking through the neighborhood with Sonia or another parish collaborator.

An exercise in self-analysis (Bourdieu 2004) is often the best way for a researcher to situate him- or herself in the social world of interest. One strategy for achieving this is to understand how the researcher is classified in this world (Mauger 1991). Classifications of this sort give meaning to the relationship that is constructed between those who live among the poor and those who analyze their world. Being able to write about this relationship allows researchers to append details of their status as researchers in a world not their own to reports of their fieldwork. Below, I share my personal experience in a self-analysis of this kind.

I would like to reflect for a moment on my relationship with Sonia to shed some light on the role of the neighborhood "gatekeeper." In October 2008, I had a conversation in the doorway of the parish church with Sonia, who liked to tell me stories about her involvement in neighborhood politics. She would remind me of how she once supported Alberto Balestrini (mayor of La Matanza, 1999–2005), but she now referred to him as "the big fish." Rosa, another church collaborator, explained that here the term had its own particular meaning: "When Sonia calls someone a big fish, she is referring to outsiders who want something from us." When I heard this, I remembered that she had once called me a "little fish." At that point, I had no idea why. Now I reminded Sonia of the nickname. She pretended not to remember having applied it to me, but then clarified: "Fishes are politicians who come in and take credit for any progress we make here. That's why people like you [scholars, university people] are little fish."

"So what about Balestrini?" I asked.

"Oh, he's a shark!" exclaimed Rosa, and we all shared a laugh.

Two months after this conversation, when the ribbon was cut on a new wing of the parish church (the story is told in chapter 5), Sonia, excited and overjoyed, told me: "There's a lot of fish swimming around here today. Big fish!"

Sonia's use of the term "fish" expressed a deep conviction that no one from outside Villa Olimpia would come into this marginalized neighborhood unless they had something of their own to gain. The big fish (Balestrini) and the little fish like me were taxonomically related: "Outsiders who want something from us." At the same time, we were also fishy, that is, arousing doubt or suspicion.

This mocking way of classifying government officials, politicians, NGO experts, social workers, university students, and church officials allowed Sonia temporarily to suspend the social hierarchies that nonetheless served as a framework of reference for her. The fact that I had entered the circle of people who knew the meaning of this category—a category used to poke fun at the neighborhood visitors behind their back—meant that I had earned her trust.

Yet the fact that she mocked the "fish" did not mean refusing to deal with them. On the contrary, her experience and her position in the neighborhood gave her social skills and contacts while versing her in the rules of the game that connected the neighborhood with the outside world. Her role as gatekeeper allowed her to accumulate social and political capital, thus distinguishing her from her neighbors. The "outsiders who want something from us" needed people on the inside to welcome them and help them obtain what they hoped to take away from here.

For Sonia, this complicity reinforced thinking and action interested in those interested (to play on Bourdieu's words). In other words, Sonia and the others had their own interests in collaborating with those who came to the neighborhood "to take something." That was my case. Although she classified me as a "little fish" and not a "big fish," Sonia never abandoned her role as the gatekeeper to Villa Olimpia who had opened the door for me to make contact with my informants. For this reason, my visits to the parish church were a ritual to reinforce Sonia's role, a role that distinguished her from her neighbors both socially and politically.

Little by little, I became aware of what being "the boy with the parish" actually meant. It was a classification that afforded me certain protection—against being robbed, for example—but also placed me on the political chessboard of Father Suárez and his collaborators. It was a classification that I had to learn to maneuver through: being recognized could prove useful, but not if that recognition changed what my informants had to share with me.

By the second month of my visits to Villa Olimpia, I had a routine: each visit to the neighborhood involved spending three or four hours in the parish church to catch up on the latest news. Later, I would take my usual walk through the neighborhood with Sonia in order to meet a new family and finally, after I had said goodbye to Sonia, I would visit some of the families I had met on earlier occasions. I rarely strayed from this routine.

In most cases, I got to the neighborhood at around 8 or 9 a.m. and stayed until the late afternoon. I rarely visited it at night. One of the reasons for this was a simple question of safety. As I explain in chapter 2, the rules of crime in the neighborhood had changed due to a spike in the use of new illegal drugs more dangerous and addictive than those of the past. It was better not to be out on the streets when the young *paco* smokers were coming out onto the corners or hanging out near the neighborhood's entry points.

Nearly 60 percent of my Villa Olimpia informants were women. This was not only because I chose to visit Villa Olimpia during the daytime, when men are generally out working. The women from Villa Olimpia also worked, but generally out of their homes, doing things like selling groceries from a gated window. The vast majority of the women who did not work were beneficiaries of some state welfare plan. This allowed them to stay at home raising their children.

For my fieldwork, it was quite useful that so many informants were welfare beneficiaries, because most had been interviewed at some point by social workers or other state officials. As a result, they were women who knew how to talk about certain aspects of their lives and were willing to respond to a wide range of questions. This accumulation of interview experiences made my contacts with the informants easier, though at times it also represented a limitation. Sometimes my informants connected with me as if I were a social worker, assuming a stereotypical role when explaining their needs, as if their acceptance as recipients of welfare depended on their story. To keep them from playing this role, I had to spark a dialogue that went beyond a list of their current needs. This meant chatting openly about a range of topics, including their taste in music, leisure activities, and personal relationships.

To strengthen the bond, make conversations natural, and keep my presence from significantly altering the routine of my informants, I only recorded conversations during my first visit. On subsequent visits, I used a notebook in which I jotted down ideas, words, and situations that I later used to record my own recollections of each meeting. The presence of the recording device allowed those interviewed to be less preoccupied with why I was there. Although I was introduced as a university professor, this introduction was not enough to dissipate all doubt. In this regard, the recorder could evoke situations more easily interpreted as, for example, a journalistic interview. For this reason, not recording was a way to make conversations more natural. Thus I only recorded my fieldwork on special occasions. For example, in chapter 5, I recount a series of speeches given by government officials visiting the neighborhood. On that occasion, the recorder was essential to reconstructing the details of each of the speeches and, since I was simply a member of an audience, had no influence on what was said.

From Politics to Money

Since an ethnographic interview must be flexible enough to adapt to the changes that can occur over the course of fieldwork, the ethnographer must also make methodological decisions that provide flexibility when utilizing theories and concepts. My fieldwork in Villa Olimpia is indicative of this process. As the process advanced, I changed the conceptual tools I employed, and this led to new decisions in how my fieldwork was organized. This theoretical and methodological flexibility led me to return to materials gathered during earlier research in order to form a new empirical basis for this book's argument.

When I arrived at Villa Olimpia, I was focused on one of the most popular topics among Argentine sociologists in the 1990s and 2000s: political clientelism. The goal was to explore the political transformations produced by neoliberalism and via clientelism. At the same time, this was connected to a sociological tradition in which political sociology took precedence over all other subdisciplines. Therefore, political clientelism gave me a topic and a subdiscipline that would ensure my producing a well-received work in my field.

Ethnography enables the broadest vision possible of people's lives. For this reason, the researcher has to pay attention to the collateral or "secondary" themes, that is, the objects that are not previously encoded as relevant for academic literature on the topic. Ethnographies allow for innovating on a given theme, giving researchers a chance to undertake an intellectual adventure. From the perspective of the dynamics of hierarchy in Argentine sociology, swapping politics for money as the key to understanding power relations represented a risk but also an opportunity. On the one hand, it was a risk to turn away from a popular topic and replace it with one that had received little attention from local sociologists. On the other hand, this gap allowed me (and obliged me) to explore innovative methodologies and conceptual formulas.

If the visits to the parish church represented the ritual that legitimated my presence in Villa Olimpia, the visits to Mary's house allowed me to delve deeper into the ethnographic perspective that ended up changing the course of my investigation and also the narrative structure of this book. These visits, which originally reflected an interest in understanding power relations through involvement in political networks, left me longing to understand how power relations were constructed through money.

The first time I visited Mary's house, during the first month of my fieldwork, I spent three hours interviewing her. During that first meeting, she shared her life story. Mary was the first person I met who actively participated in Salcedo's political network. In addition, she was willing to talk with me and introduce me to the rest of her family. One of the reasons for this willingness is that Mary was also vying to become a "gatekeeper" for new visitors to Villa Olimpia. It was a way of obtaining social and political distinction among the other residents. Mary had learned this role by watching Sonia and other members of Salcedo's political network.

By spending hours at a time with Mary, and accompanying her on her own visits, I reached a more comprehensive understanding of her household economy, gradually realizing that politics was only one dimension of the multiple social orders on which her survival depended. Through the perspective of the sociology of money, I was able to embrace the heterogeneous aspects of the economic life of the poor, reconstructing the power relations that took shape as money circulated. Moreover, since Mary now knew me well enough to speak openly about most everything, money was a topic she mentioned with regard to almost every other aspect of everyday life—a life conditioned by constant financial stress.

When I took inventory of that first month of fieldwork, I decided to shift the focus of my analysis from politics to money. As a result, I began guiding my informants—whom I was getting to know better and better—towards topics associated with the circulation of money. This change in focus meant modifying my fieldwork. First of all, I decided to explore how money had come up with my informants in the interviews I had already conducted, even though at that point it had not been my main focus. This rereading helped me ensure that I was on the right track by redefining my research topic, inasmuch as I noted that, implicitly or explicitly, money appeared time and again in everyday accounts of Villa Olimpia. As had been the case in my interactions with Mary and her family, the interviews with my other informants also revealed money's central role in their lives. Besides visiting the parish church and Mary's house during every visit, I also started searching for new contacts—like neighborhood retailers—who would provide additional insight into the money dynamics in Villa Olimpia. Although not all the testimonies of these informants made their way into this book, they all helped me form the spine of my argument. In this regard, I sought out individuals whose everyday activities involved different social orders and pieces of money. To find such people, snowball sampling was critical (mainly through the parish church), though it also depended on how available informants were when it came to establishing a somewhat long-term bond (by periodical visits to their homes).

Choosing a new research topic led me to additional research outside Villa Olimpia. I had already been with Mary and other members of Salcedo's political network to marches or rallies organized to support the national government. Now I left the neighborhood with Mary and other locals when they went shopping; I was interested in understanding their consumer logic. In this regard, the perspective of the Villa Olimpia inhabitants did not suffice: the viewpoint of the retailers who interacted with them was also essential. For this reason, I added a new stage of fieldwork in November and December 2009. During this period, I interviewed retailers in neighborhoods close to Villa Olimpia and also obtained material from a survey on consumer lending in two retail areas a few miles from Villa Olimpia. I did approximately ten interviews in San Justo and another ten at CyC (Crovara y Cristianía) in addition to the survey, whose sample included a hundred adult men and women living in poor neighborhoods like Villa Olimpia (see chapter 1).

In conclusion, using money as the tool of my theoretical analysis enabled a comprehensive interpretation of the world of the poor, one that takes into account the vast differences between existing social orders and the way the limits between these orders are negotiated. Instead of analyzing only a fragment of the lives of the poor—politics, religion, family, and so on—I focus on how money connects them. Money became the vehicle that took me deep into the world of the poor, into homes, shops, markets, drug houses, political party offices, and churches to see how these different sites are connected by money and also by the ideas and feelings associated with money. The circulation of money thus became a medium for exploring the power dynamics that characterize the heterogeneous social bonds and sites of the poor.

Before and After My Fieldwork in Villa Olimpia

The majority of the empirical materials that allowed me to develop the core argument of this book came from my fieldwork in Villa Olimpia. The decision to change the focus of my investigation not only had an impact on the way I conducted my fieldwork in Villa Olimpia, but also obliged me to reinterpret previous research from a new perspective. In this regard, the materials from two previous investigations I had done—one on homeless people selling a magazine published by an NGO and another on an urban recycling co-operative—both enriched the analysis of my book.

These empirical materials helped me to enhance the theoretical concepts presented in this book. These two investigations, conducted between 2004 and 2006, targeted alternative work systems developed by people excluded from the job market. I used these materials to supplement my argument in chapter 3 on *donated* money. The first was an ethnographic study of homeless people selling a street magazine and their interactions with buyers; over the course of four months in 2004, I accompanied the vendors to different areas of downtown Buenos Aires. As part of my analysis, I also focused on the content of the magazines themselves, especially the letters to the editor. I was interested in understanding the exchanges between the people living on the streets who had developed this alternative type of job and their buyers, generally men and women from the urban middle classes.

For the second investigation that supplements the argument of this book, I spent six months in 2006 analyzing the interactions between members of a recycling co-op and middle-class residents in the district of La Matanza. The co-op members came from marginal neighborhoods near Villa Olimpia, and none of them had formal employment. The local recycling program provided an alternative source of income. In this case, I conducted an ethnographic study, accompanying the recyclers on their routes and seeing how they interacted with the residents of the Morales neighborhood.

To supplement my argument in chapter 1, I incorporated an income-and-spending study of eight families that had previously lived in a slum south of the city of Buenos Aires; all eight had moved into new homes built as part of a state housing program. I conducted this study in November 2001 as part of an investigation on new forms of consumer purchasing and lending among the poor (Wilkis 2014). The study consisted of three meetings with each family. In the first meeting, I did a semi-structured interview on the employment, housing, and educational histories of each member of the household and left them a spreadsheet where they could enter the household's daily income and expenditures. One week later, I returned to pick up the spreadsheet and do an interview about the entries. Two weeks later, I held a third meeting to discuss household strategies for financing consumer purchases in greater detail.

Finally, I want to mention some journalistic materials that also contributed to the argument of this book. In chapter 2, I cite a story that I co-wrote with a journalist on the enormous informal market La Salada. To show how money *donated* by the state is suspicious, Chapter 3 includes an editorial that I wrote in one of Argentina's national newspapers and the reactions of the paper's readership in the form of online comments.

The final lesson of these notes on fieldwork methodology is to be found in these very lines. By actively reflecting on the research process, investigators are better able to control for the chance occurrences that research, writing, and indeed all acts of sociological thought involve. This appendix not only takes the reader behind the scenes of the investigation but has also allowed me as an author to journey through my own experience. As an author, it is important to realize that there are both personal and impersonal aspects to any research process. The writing of this book depended on decisions I made as an author, but also on factors associated with the academic field in which I am immersed. In the case of this book, I would add, these factors also emerge from the international exchange between academic institutions in core and peripheral countries. There are certain ways of thinking and writing that are required for ideas in sociology to circulate from one academic universe to another. Like any book in sociology, *The Moral Power of Money* is the synthesis of two histories, one biographical and one institutional.

Notes

Introduction

1. Peronism is the political movement that has been historically associated with the Argentine poor since its founding in the 1940s by three-time president (1946–51; 1951–55; 1973–74) Juan Domingo Perón. When the party was founded, its political agenda included defending workers and their rights, promoting state intervention in the economy, and defending national industry. Peronism depended on strong, charismatic leadership and the support of industrial and farm workers, small and medium-sized business owners, and certain other sectors of the urban middle classes. The party managed to survive even the death of its founder, Perón, and perhaps more surprisingly, a Peronist administration headed by President Carlos Menem (1989–99), which implemented sweeping neoliberal policies nationwide. Presidents Néstor Kirchner and Cristina Fernández de Kirchner have been the most recent Peronist leaders, and as a power couple in Peronism, they evoked the party's founder, Juan Domingo Perón, and his popular wife Eva Duarte de Perón.

2. For a list of reviews and other articles about the book see www.portfoliosoftthepoor.com/media.asp (accessed March 26, 2017).

3. In Brazil, similar processes led to the appearance of a "new middle class" formed by the nearly forty million people who had escaped poverty and accessed the consumer market thanks to the redistribution policies implemented by President Lula da Silva (Oliven and Pinheiro Machado 2012).

4. In the appendix, I provide a detailed description of my fieldwork methodology.

Chapter 1

1. To compare this process with that of other countries in Latin America, like Chile, see Ossandón 2012.

2. Source: Central Bank of Argentina.

3. The use of credit cards in Argentina tripled between 2004 and 2011, from five to fourteen million credit cards nationwide.

4. This point is worth noting, given the growing interest among both scholars and politicians in microcredit programs organized by the government, NGOs, and multilateral credit agencies (Schuster 2015).

5. For the episodes of 1989, see Salvatore 1995 and Neufeld and Cravino 2001; for those of 2001, see Auyero 2007.

Chapter 2

1. www.forbes.com/sites/megacities/2011/03/28/la-salada-the-largest-informal-market-in-south-america/#381e85143174 (accessed March 28, 2017).

2. *Paco* is an extremely cheap and highly addictive drug made from the residual coca paste base of hydrochloride of cocaine, combined with sulfuric acid and kerosene, with devastating consequences for users.

3. See Gutiérrez 2004 for a succinct summary of such survival strategies.

4. Few of my informants admitted to making use of *fiado*, or access to informal credit that involved no paperwork other than an entry in the grocer's ledger. The negative associations and stigma associated with this lending scheme were clear. In one of my first visits to Villa Olimpia, I was surprised to hear Father Suárez say, "Buying at a large supermarket sets you free—you're no longer a slave to the neighborhood grocery." Many other people said similar things to indicate that *fiado* absorbs all of a person's money, although they had done it at some point, especially at the local grocery, "when things weren't going too well." The logic was associated with critical economic situations in which the neighborhood merchants received more customers than ever. In 2003, eight out of ten grocery stores sold on *fiado* according to a survey of nearly seven thousand stores (Di Nucci and Lan 2007). These data are indicative of how grocery stores took a percentage of retail sales away from large supermarkets in the crisis after 2001. During this period, by offering informal retail credit, these small groceries gave shoppers added value. This added value has been highlighted in historic analyses of *pulperías* and general stores (Mayo 2007). Its persistence shows how important credit can be in building clientele among the poor, as also shown in studies done in other countries (Caplovitz 1967; Villarreal 2000; Avanza, Laferté and Penissat 2006; Fontaine 2008).

5. "There was a young man who I sold to on credit. He had run up quite a tab and then his son was born with a medical condition. How could I possibly ask him to pay me back? I couldn't. Then he came and paid me. . . . The girl who lives across the street told me things weren't going very well at her job and she couldn't pay me now, but that she would pay me as soon as she could," Marga recounted.

Chapter 3

1. *New York Times*, January 3, 2011.

2. To lend support to this argument, I also made use of ethnographic materials gathered before my fieldwork in Villa Olimpia. By temporarily shifting away from my ethnography in this neighborhood during this specific period, I was able to reveal how the pieces of money function in heterogeneous contexts and how these pieces are analytically connected by a certain approach to money. The methodological appendix describes the fieldwork I did during this prior research.

3. Since the 1990s, in many cities in Latin American and across the world, organizations of homeless people have published a journal or magazine as a way to get off the street, recover from addiction, and combat other social vulnerabilities. The sellers get a portion of their sales. At the beginning of the year 2000, there were 150 organizations of this kind around the world.

4. Between 2000 and 2004, around 1,800 people signed up to sell the magazine. The majority were men (73.3 percent), living mainly on the street (32.9 percent), in lodging houses (23.5 percent), and in shelters run by the municipal government (7.5 percent).

5. "Face is an image of self delineated in terms of approved social attributes. . . . A person who can maintain face in the current situation is someone who abstained from certain actions in the past that would have been difficult to face up to later" (Goffman 1970, 13–19).

6. This district is located to the west of the city of Buenos Aires. Due to its large size and population (nearly two million people), it acquires the political dimension of the largest provinces in the country. The first suburbanization in which outlying neighborhoods were consolidated within the capital city was followed by a second process in which a peripheral strip of districts was formed in greater Buenos Aires (Torres 1975). This process was linked to a shift in the migrants coming into the city (internal migrants had replaced those arriving from abroad) and to Argentina's industrialization process (import substitution) in the 1940s. La Matanza became a magnet for both industries and for workers, leading this town to be called a "workers' city" (Manzano 2009). However, the processes of deindustrialization that started in the 1970s changed the social and urban structure. Of the twelve thousand industries existing in the mid-1970s, some four thousand remained in 2013 (Agostino, 2003). In 2006, the unemployment rate in the most relegated areas reached 32.1 percent. Around 40 percent of employed residents worked as unqualified labor and domestic servants. In terms of welfare, 67.8 percent of the employed residents received no assistance whatsoever. Poverty in the country averaged 48.9 percent but reached 63.8 percent in the most relegated area (*Living Conditions Survey*, county of La Matanza 2007).

7. The incompetence of the private trash pickup service contributed to this.

8. In March 2008, in response to a decree that increased the tax-withholding percentages of the agricultural sector, protests led by farmers began across the country. The conflict lasted nearly four months with lock-outs, roadblocks, and mass protests in cities like Rosario and Buenos Aires. The government and its political allies also organized rallies and actions to support the government's decision. Ultimately, the decree was not enacted.

9. In certain cases, a middleman can facilitate access to government welfare plans. Political leaders in poor neighborhoods use their influence and contacts in state offices to help get residents on the roster. The exchanges between political bosses and inhabitants of marginalized neighborhoods are marked by this informal dynamic. (Auyero 2001).

Chapter 4

1. Both typical foods of Paraguay; *chipá* is a small cheese-filled roll and *sopa paraguaya* is similar to cornbread.

2. Most slums are not connected to the domestic gas network and thus must use gas canisters for heating and cooking. After paying a relatively hefty sum for the canister, users only pay a refilling charge.

3. A street performance particularly popular among the lower classes. Many neighborhoods have their own *murgas* that perform during the summer months and Carnival season. Drummers play and blow whistles, while others dance. All wear colorful costumes and people of all ages participate.

4. Marcel Mauss, comments following a paper by François Simiand, "La monnaie, réalité sociale," *Annales sociologiques,* ser. D, 1 (1934): 61.

Chapter 5

1. Bellardi and de Paula (1986) offer an accurate depiction of this slum-eradication process.

2. Mujica, an Argentine member of the Movement of Third World Priests, was killed coming out of mass by a right-wing para-police group in 1974. Sonia was very proud to have known Father Mujica and shared details about her friendship with the priest's sister.

3. "Sacrifice is a means to allow the layman to communicate with the sacred through a victim" (Hubert and Mauss 1970).

4. The Virgen de Luján, a local Marian devotion, is worshipped throughout Argentina.

5. Evita, Juan Perón's second wife, María Eva Duarte de Perón (1919–52), prominent in Peronist iconography, is associated with the heyday of workers' rights.

6. Pedro Bonifacio Palacios (1854–1917), the poet known as Almafuerte, was

one of Argentina's first literary figures to both come from humble origins and celebrate the underlings of society.

Chapter 6

1. The expansion of informal rental markets has become a source of income for many inhabitants of marginalized neighborhoods. Cravino (2007) analyzes this process in the slums of Buenos Aires, as Abramo (2003) does for the favelas of Rio de Janeiro.

2. There is a wide range of literature on the role of women in managing the finances of poor families covering different regions and historic periods. For preindustrial Europe, see Fontaine 2008; in the United States at the start of the twentieth and twenty-first centuries, see Zelizer 1994; in Africa, Guerrin 2010; in Mexico, Villarreal 2009; and in Argentina, Geldstein 2009.

3. In an ethnographic study on the money of women traders in Potosí, Bolivia, Pascale Absi (2007) analyzes the separation of money in multiple change purses, whose purpose is to turn sales into savings.

4. See chapter 3, n. 8.

5. In Latin American countries, a daughter's fifteenth birthday is something akin to a sweet sixteen celebration and often involves a party for family and friends as lavish as a wedding.

6. Due to the consistent instability of Argentine currency, purchasing dollars has been a traditional method for saving money among all the country's social classes.

References

Abramo, Pedro. 2003. "La teoría económica de la favela: Cuatro notas sobre la localización residencial de los pobres y el mercado inmobiliario informal." *Revista Ciudad y Territorios* 35: 273–94.

Absi, Pascale. 2007. "Il ne faut pas mélanger les fortunes: Travail, genre et revenus chez les commerçantes de Potosí." In *Turbulences monétaires et sociales: L'Amérique latine dans une perspective comparée*, ed. Valeria Hernández, Pépita Ould-Ahmed, Jean Papail, and Pascal Phélinas, 355–93. Paris: L'Harmattan.

Aglietta, Michel, and André Orléan. 1982. *La violence de la monnaie*. Paris: Presses Universitaires de France.

Agostino, Hilda. 2003. *El partido de La Matanza: Aportes para comenzar a conocerlo*. Buenos Aires: Junta de Estudios Históricos, Geográficos y Estadísticos del Partido de La Matanza.

Alexander, Jeffrey C. 1995. *Fin de Siècle Social Theory: Relativism, Reduction, and the Problem of Reason*. New York: Verso. Translated by Nathalie Zaccaï-Reyners as *La réduction: Critique de Bourdieu* (Paris: Éd. du Cerf, 2000).

Altimir, Oscar, and Luis A. Beccaria. 1999. *El mercado de trabajo bajo el nuevo régimen económico en Argentina*. Santiago de Chile: CEPAL.

Anderson, Elijah. 1999. *Code of the Street: Decency, Violence and the Moral Life of the Inner City*. New York: Norton.

Aspers, Patrik, and Nigel Dodd, eds. 2015. *Re-imagining Economic Sociology*. Oxford: Oxford University Press.

Auyero, Javier. 2001. *Poor People's Politics: Peronist Survival Networks and the Legacy of Evita*. Durham, NC: Duke University Press.

———. 2007. *Routine Politics and Violence in Argentina: The Gray Zone of State Power*. New York: Cambridge University Press.

Avanza, Martina, Gilles Laferté, and Étienne Penissat. 2006. "O crédito entre as classes populares francesas: O exemplo de uma loja em Lens." *Revista Mana* 12 (1): 7–38.

Bandelj, Nina. 2012. "Relational Work and Economic Sociology." *Politics and Society* 40: 175–201.

Bayón, Cristina, and Gonzalo Saraví. 2002. "Vulnerabilidad social en la Argentina de los años noventa: Impactos de la crisis en el Gran Buenos Aires." In *Trabajo y ciudadanía: Los cambiantes rostros de la integración y exclusión social en cuatro áreas metropolitanas de América Latina*, ed. Rúben Kaztman and Guillermo Wormald, 61–132. [Montevideo, Uruguay]: CEBRA.

Becker, Howard. 1997. *Outsiders: Studies in the Sociology of Deviance*. New York: Free Press.

Beckert, Jens, and Frank Wehinger. 2012. "In the Shadow: Illegal Markets and Economic Sociology." *Socio-economic Review* 11 (1): 5–30.

Bellardi, Marta, and Aldo de Paula. 1986. *Villas miserias: Origen, erradicación y respuestas populares*. Buenos Aires: Centro Editor de América Latina.

Biggart, Nicole. 2001. "Banking on Each Other: The Situational Logic of Rotating Savings and Credits Associations." *Advances in Qualitative Organization Research* 3: 129–54.

Blanc, Jérôme. 2009. "Usages de l'argent et pratiques monétaires." In *Traité de sociologie économique*, ed. Phillipe Steiner and François Vatin, 649–88. Paris: Presses Universitaires de France.

Bloch, Maurice, and Jonathan Parry. 1989. "Introduction." In *Money and the Morality of Exchange*, ed. Bloch and Parry, 1–32. New York: Cambridge University Press.

Boltanski, Luc, and Laurent Thévenot. 2006. *On Justification: Economies of Worth*. Princeton, NJ: Princeton University Press.

Borges, Antonádia. 2003. *Tempo de Brasília*. Rio de Janeiro: Relume Dumará.

Bourdieu, Pierre. 1977. *Algérie 60: Structures économiques et structures temporelles*. Paris: Éd. de Minuit.

———. 1984. *Distinction: A Social Critique of the Judgement of Taste*. Cambridge, MA: Harvard University Press. Originally published as *La distinction: Critique sociale du jugement* (Paris: Éd. de Minuit, 1979).

———. 1990. *The Logic of Practice*. Stanford, CA: Stanford University Press.

———. 1996. "On the Family as a Realized Category." *Theory, Culture & Society* 13: 19–26.

———. 2000. *Pascalian Meditations*. Stanford, CA: Stanford University Press.

———. 2004. *Science of Science and Reflexivity*. Chicago: University of Chicago Press.

———. 2005. *The Social Structures of the Economy*. Cambridge: Polity Press.

Bourdieu, Pierre (dir.), Luc Boltanski, and J.-C. Chamboredon. 1963. "La banque et sa clientèle: Éléments d'une sociologie du crédit." MS. Paris: Centre de Sociologie Européenne.

Bourgois, Philippe. 2003. *In Search of Respect: Selling Crack in El Barrio*. New York: Cambridge University Press.

Brakarz, José. 2002. *Ciudades para todos: La experiencia reciente en programas para mejoramiento de barrios*. Washington, DC: Inter-American Development Bank.

Caillé, Alain. 1994. *Don, interêt et désintéressement: Bourdieu, Mauss, Platon et quelques autres*. Paris: Éd. la Découverte / Mauss.

Callon, Michel. 1998. "Introduction: The Embeddedness of Economic Markets in Economics." In *The Laws of the Markets*, ed. Callon, 1–57. Malden, MA: Blackwell.

Callon, Michel, and Koray Çalişkan. 2009. "Economization. Part 1: Shifting Attention from the Economy towards Processes of Economization." *Economy and Society* 38 (3): 369–98.

Calvo, Ernesto, and Victoria Murillo. 2004. "Who Delivers? Partisan Clients in the Argentine Electoral Market." *American Journal of Political Science* 48: 742–57.

Caplovitz, David. 1967. *The Poor Pay More: Consumer Practices of Low-Income Families*. New York: Free Press of Glencoe.

Carruthers, Bruce G., and Laura Ariovich. 2010. *Money and Credit: A Sociological Approach*. Cambridge: Polity Press.

Chesnais, François, ed. 2004. *La finance mondialisée: Racines sociales et politiques, configuration, conséquences*. Paris: Éd. la Découverte.

Cogliandro, Gisell. 2010. "El programa Asignación Universal por Hijo para Protección Social y los cambios en los Programas de Transferencias Condicionadas." Buenos Aires: Fundación Siena.

Collins, Darryl, Jonathan Murdoch, Stuart Rutherford, and Orlando Ruthven. 2009. *Portfolios of the Poor: How the World's Poor Live on $2 a Day*. Princeton, NJ: Princeton University Press.

Corcuff, Philippe. 2003. *Bourdieu autrement—fragilités d'un sociologue de combat*. Paris: Textuel, 2003.

Cravino, María Cristina. 2007. *Las villas de la ciudad: Mercado e informalidad urbana*. Buenos Aires: Universidad Nacional de General Sarmiento.

Delfini, Marcelo, and Valentina Pichetti. 2005. "Desigualdad y pobreza en Argentina en los noventa." *Revista Política y Cultura* 24: 187–206

Deville, Joe. 2015. *Lived Economies of Default: Consumer Credit, Debt Collection, and the Capture of Affect*. London: Routledge

Dewey, Matias. 2012. "Illegal Police Protection and the Market for Stolen Vehicles in Buenos Aires." *Journal of Latin American Studies* 44: 679–702.

Di Nucci, Josefina, and Diana Lan. 2007. "Cambios en la distribución minorista de alimentos y bebidas en Argentina 2001–2003: Hacia nuevas horizontalidades territoriales." *Geograficando* 3 (3): 129–49.

Dodd, Nigel. 2014. *The Social Life of Money.* Princeton, NJ: Princeton University Press.

D'Onofrio, Federico. 2008. "Creditos al consumo tras la crisis: El boom del consumer finance en Argentina." MA diss., Universidad Nacional de Mar del Plata.

Dumont, Louis. 1966. *Homo hierarchicus: Le système des castes et ses implications.* Paris: Gallimard.

Durkheim, Émile. 2011 [1912]. *The Elementary Forms of Religious Life.* Oxford: Oxford University Press.

Elias, Norbert. 1983. *The Court Society.* Oxford: Blackwell.

Elias, Norbert, and John Scotson. 1994. *The Established and the Outsiders: A Sociological Enquiry into Community Problems.* London: Sage.

Elyachar, Julia. 2005. *Markets of Dispossession: NGOs, Economic Development and the State in Cairo.* Durham, NC: Duke University Press.

———. 2012. "Next Practices: Knowledge, Infrastructure, and Public Goods at the Bottom of the Pyramid." *Public Culture* 24 (1): 109–29.

Fassin, Didier. 2000. "La supplique: Stratégies rhétoriques et constructions identitaires dans les demandes d'aide d'urgence." *Annales: Histoire, Sciences Sociales* 19 (5): 955–81.

Ferguson, James. 2015. *Give a Man a Fish: Reflections on the New Politics of Distribution.* Durham, NC: Duke University Press.

FETIA–CTA. 2005. "Características de la desindustrialización en la Argentina durante las últimas décadas." http://archivo.cta.org.ar/Caracteristicas-de-la.html (accessed May 25, 2017).

Figueiro, Pablo. 2013. *Lógicas sociales del consumo: El gasto improductivo en un asentamiento bonaerense.* Buenos Aires: Unsam Edita.

Fonseca, Claudia. 2000. *Família, fofoca e honra: Etnografia de relaçoes de gênero e violência em grupos populares.* Porto Alegre, RS, Brazil: Editora da Universidade, Universidade Federal do Rio Grande do Sul.

Fontaine, Laurence. 2008. *L'économie morale: Pauvreté, crédit et confiance dans l'Europe préindustrielle.* Paris: Gallimard.

Forni, Floreal H., and Graciela Gómez. 2002. "Entre cruces y galpones: La religión de los pobres en los barrios del conurbano." In *De la exclusión a la organización: Hacia la integración de los pobres en los nuevos barrios del conurbano bonaerense,* ed. Forni. Buenos Aires: Ediciones CICCUS.

Fourcade, Marion, and Kieran Healy. 2007. "The Views of Moral Markets." *Annual Review of Sociology* 33: 285–311.

Franco, Rolando. 1996. "Los paradigmas de la política social en América Latina." *Revista de la CEPAL* 58: 9–22.

Frederic, Sabina. 2004. *Buenos vecinos, malos políticos: Moralidad y política en el Gran Buenos Aires*. Buenos Aires: Prometeo Libros.

Gago, Verónica. 2012. "La Salada: ¿Un caso de globalización desde abajo?" *Revista Nueva Sociedad* 241: 63–78.

Garfinkel, Harold. 1956. "Conditions of Successful Degradation Ceremonies." *American Journal of Sociology* 61 (5): 420–24.

Gaxie, Daniel. 2005. "Retribution du militantisme et paradoxes de l'action colective." *Swiss Political Science Review* 1 (1): 157–88.

Geertz, Clifford. 1962. "The Rotating Credit Association: A 'Middle Rung' in Development." *Economic Development and Cultural Change* 10 (3): 241–63.

Geldstein, Rosa. 2004. "De 'buenas' madres y 'malos' proveedores: Género y trabajo en la reestructuración económica." *Subjetividad y Procesos Cognitivos* 5: 126–55.

Girón, Ignacio. 2011. *La Salada: Radiografía de la feria más polémica de Latinoamérica*. Buenos Aires: Ediciones B.

Goffman, Erving. 1970. *Ritual de la interacción*. Buenos Aires: Editorial Tiempo Contemporáneo.

———. 1983. "The Interaction Order: American Sociological Association, 1982 Presidential Address." *American Sociological Review* 48 (1) (February): 1–17.

Goldstein, Donna. 2003. *Laughter Out of Place: Race, Class, Violence, and Sexuality in a Rio Shantytown*. Berkeley: University of California Press.

Graeber, David. 2011. *Debt: The First 5,000 Years*. New York: Melville House.

Gregory, Chris. 2012. "On Money Debt and Morality: Some Reflections on the Contribution of Economic Anthropology." *Social Anthropology* 20 (4): 380–96.

Guber, Rosana. 1984. "Identidad social villera: Resignificación de un estigma." *Runa* 32: 81–100.

Guérin, Isabelle. 2010. "Las mujeres pobres y su dinero: Entre la supervivencia cotidiana, la vida privada, las obligaciones familiares y las normas sociales." *La Ventana* 32 (4): 7–51.

Guérin, Isabelle, Sólene Morvant-Roux, and Magdalena Villarreal, eds. 2014. *Microfinance, Debt and Over-indebteness: Juggling with Money*. New York: Routledge.

Guseva, Alya. 2008. *Into the Red: The Birth of the Credit Card Market in Postcommunist Russia*. Stanford, CA: Stanford University Press.

Gutiérrez, Alicia B. 2004. *Pobre', como siempre: Estrategias de reproducción social en la pobreza; Un estudio de caso*. Córdoba, Argentina: Ferreyra.

Guyer, Jane I. 2004. *Marginal Gains: Monetary Transactions in Atlantic Africa*. Chicago: University of Chicago Press.

———. 2012. "Soft Currencies, Cash Economies, New Monies: Past and Present." *PNAS* 109: 2214–21.

———. 2016. "Translator's Introduction: The Gift That Keeps On Giving." In Marcel Mauss, *The Gift*. Chicago: University of Chicago Press.

190 References

Hacher, Sebastían. 2011. *Sangre salada: Una feria en los márgenes*. Buenos Aires: Editorial Marea.

Hakim, Catherine. 2010. "Erotic Capital." *European Sociological Review* 26 (5): 499–518.

Hanlon, Joseph, Armando Barrientos, and David Hulme. 2010. *Just Give Money to the Poor: The Development Revolution from the South*. Sterling, VA: Kumarian Press.

Harvey, David. 2005. *A Brief History of Neoliberalism*. Oxford: Oxford University Press.

Hitlin, Steven, and Stephen Vaisey. 2010. "Back to the Future." In *The Handbook of Sociology of Morality*, ed. Hitlin and Vaisey, 3–14. New York: Springer.

Honneth, Axel. 1996. *The Struggle for Recognition: The Moral Grammar of Social Conflicts*. Cambridge, MA: MIT Press.

Hornes, Martín. 2014. "Transferencias condicionadas y sentidos plurales: El dinero estatal en la economía de los hogares argentinos." *Revista de Antropología y Arqueología Antípoda* 18: 61–83.

Hubert, Henri, and Marcel Mauss. 1970 [1906]. "Introducción al análisis a algunos fenómenos religiosos." In Mauss, *Obras Completas I*. Barcelona: Barral.

Informe Encuesta Nacional de Gastos de Hogar. 2014. Buenos Aires: Centro de Estudios Sociales de la Economia.

James, Deborah. 2015. *Money from Nothing: Indebtedness and Aspiration in South Africa*. Stanford, CA: Stanford University Press.

Janoschka, Michael. 2002. "El nuevo modelo de la ciudad latinoamericana: Fragmentación y privatización." *Revista EURE* 28 (85): 11–20.

Karim, Lamia. 2011. *Microfinance and Its Discontents: Women in Debt in Bangladesh*. Minneapolis: University of Minnesota Press

Karsenti, Bruno. 1994. *Marcel Mauss: Le fait social total*. Paris: Presses Universitaires de France.

Kessler, Gabriel. 2002. "De proveedores, amigos, vecinos y *barderos*: Acerca de trabajo, delito y sociabilidad en jóvenes del Gran Buenos Aires." In *Sociedad y sociabilidad en la Argentina de los 90*, ed. Silvio Feldam, Miguel Murmis, et al., 137–70. Buenos Aires: Biblos.

———. 2014. *Controversias sobre la desigualdad*. Buenos Aires: Fondo de Cultura Ecónomica.

Klein, Naomi. 2008. *The Shock Doctrine: The Rise of Disaster Capitalism*. New York: Picador.

Knight, Frank. 1921. *Risk, Uncertainty and Profit*. Boston: Houghton Mifflin.

Kuroda, Akinubo. 2008. "Concurrent but Non-integrable Currency Circuits: Complementary Relationships among Monies in Modern China and Other Regions." *Financial History Review* 15: 17–36.

Langley, Paul. 2008. *The Everyday Life of Global Finance: Saving and Borrowing in Anglo-America.* Oxford: Oxford University Press.

Lapavitsas, Costas. 2007. "Information and Trust as Social Aspects of Credit." *Economy and Society* 36 (3): 416–36.

Lazar, Sian. 2008. *El Alto, Rebel City: Self and Citizenship in Andean Bolivia.* Durham, NC: Duke University Press.

Lazaratto, Maurizio. 2011. *La fabrique de l'homme endetté: Essai sur la condition néolibérale.* Paris: Éd. Amsterdam.

Lazarus, Jeanne. 2011. *L'épreuve de l'argent: Banques, banquiers, clients.* Paris: Calmann-Lévy.

Levitsky, Steven. 2003. *Transforming Labor-Based Parties in Latin America: Argentine Peronism in Comparative Perspective.* New York: Cambridge University Press.

Levitsky, Steven, and Kenneth Roberts, eds. 2011. *The Resurgence of the Latin American Left.* Baltimore: Johns Hopkins University Press.

Linhardt, Dominique. 2012. "Avant-propos: Épreuves d'État; Une variation sur la définition wébérienne de l'État." *Quaderni* 78: 5–22.

Lins Ribeiro, Gustavo. 2012. "Globalization from Below and the Non-hegemonic World-System." In *Globalization from Below: The World's Other Economy,* ed. Gordon Mathews, Gustavo Lins Ribeiro, and Carlos Alba Vega, 221–35. New York: Routledge.

Lomnitz, Larissa Adler de. 1975. *Cómo sobreviven los marginados.* Mexico City: Siglo Veintiuno. Translated as *Networks and Marginality: Life in a Mexican Shantytown* (New York: Academic Press, 1977).

Manzano, Virginia. 2009. "'Piquetes' y acción estatal en Argentina: Un análisis etnográfico de la configuración de procesos políticos." In *Estado y movimientos sociales: Estudios etnográficos en Argentina y Brasil,* ed. Mabel Grimberg, María Ines Fernández Álvarez, and Marcelo Carvalho Rosa, 15–36. Buenos Aires: Editorial Antropofagia.

Marron, Donchan. 2007. "Lending by Numbers: Credit Scoring and the Constitution of Risk within American Consumer Credit." *Economy and Society* 36 (1): 103–33.

Marx, Karl. 1976 [1867]. *Capital: A Critique of Political Economy.* London: Penguin Books.

Mauger, Gérard. 1991. "Enquêter en milieu populaire." *Revue Genèses* 6: 125–34.

———. 2001. "Précarisation et nouvelles formes d'encadrement des classes populaires. " *Actes de la recherche en sciences sociales* 136: 3–4.

———. 2006. *Les bandes, le milieu et la bohème populaire: Études de sociologie de la déviance des jeunes des classes populaires, 1975–2005.* Paris: Belin.

Maurer, Bill. 2012. "The Disunity of Finance: Alternative Practices to Western Finance." In *The Oxford Handbook of the Sociology of Finance,* ed. Katherine Knorr-Cetina and Alex Preda, 413–30. Oxford: Oxford University Press.

Mauss, Marcel. 2000 [1954]. *The Gift: The Form and Reason for Exchange in Archaic Societies.* New York: Norton.

Maxwell, Cameron, and Eric Hershberg, coord. 2010. *Latin America's Left Turn: Politics, Policies and Trajectories of Change.* Boulder, CO: Lynne Rienner.

Mayo, Carlos. 2007. *Mostradores, clientes y fiados.* Mar del Plata, Argentina: Ediciones Suárez.

McFall, Liz. 2014. *Devising Consumption: Cultural Economies of Insurance, Credit and Spending.* New York: Routledge.

Mehta, Jal, and Christopher Winship. 2010. "Moral Power." In *The Handbook of Sociology of Morality,* ed. Steven Hitlin and Stephen Vaisey, 425–38. New York: Springer.

Merchiers, Jacques. 2004. "Y a-t-il des dispositions morales?" *Année Sociologique* 54: 455–81.

Miller, Daniel. 1998. *A Theory of Shopping.* Ithaca, NY: Cornell University Press.

Mills, C. Wright. 2000 [1959]. *The Sociological Imagination.* Oxford: Oxford University Press.

Muldrew, Craig. 1998. *The Economy of Obligation: The Culture of Credit and Social Relations in Early Modern England.* New York: St. Martin's Press.

Muller, Lucia. 2009. "'Então, eu fui à luta!' Repensando as representações e práticas econômicas de grupos populares a partir de uma trajetória de ascensão social." *Política/Sociedade* 8 (15): 145–71.

Neiburg, Federico. 2016. "A True Coin of their Dreams: Imaginary Moneis in Haiti." *Hau: Journal of Ethnographic Theory* 6(1): 73–95.

Nelms, Taylor. 2015. "Taylor Nelms reseña y discute 'Las sospechas del dinero de Ariel Wilkis.'" *Estudios de la Economía.* https://estudiosdelaeconomia.wordpress.com/2014/12/01/taylor-nelms-resena-y-discute-las-sospechas-del-dinero-de-ariel-wilkis (accessed March 26, 2017).

Neufeld, Maria Rosa, and Maria Cristina Cravino. 2001. "Los saqueos y las ollas populares de 1989 en el Gran Buenos Aires: Pasado y presente de una experiencia formativa." *Revista de Antropología* 44 (2): 147–72.

O'Donnell, Guillermo. 1996. "Illusions about Consolidation." *Journal of Democracy* 7: 34–51.

———. 1999. "Delegative Democracy." In *Counterpoints: Selected Essays on Authoritarianism and Democratization,* ed. O'Donnell, 159–74. Notre Dame, IN: University of Notre Dame Press.

Orléan, Andre. 2009. "La sociologie économique de la monnaie." In *Traité de sociologie économique,* ed. Philippe Steiner and François Vatin, 209–46. Paris: Presses Universitaires de France.

Ortiz, Horacio. 2013. "Financial Value: Economic, Moral, Political, Global." *HAU: Journal of Ethnographic Theory* 3 (1): 64–79.

Ossandón, José, ed. 2012. *Destapando la caja negra: Sociologias de los créditos de con-*

sume en Chile. Santiago de Chile: Instituto de Investigacion en Ciencias Sociales, Universidad Diego Portales.

Ossona, Jorge. 2014. *Punteros, malandras y porongas: Ocupación de tierras y usos políticos de la pobreza.* Buenos Aires: Siglo Veintiuno Argentina.

Paiva, Veronica, and Mariano Perelman. 2008. "Recuperación y recolección informal de residuos: La perspectiva de la teoría ambiental y las políticas públicas, Ciudad de Buenos Aires, 2001–2007." *Cuaderno Urbano* 2: 35–54.

Partenio, Florencia. 2009. "Género y participación política: Los desafíos de la organización de las mujeres dentro del movimiento piquetero en Argentina." Informe final del concurso: Las deudas abiertas de América Latina y el Caribe. Buenos Aires: CLACSO–ASDI. http://bibliotecavirtual.clacso.org.ar/ar/libros/becas/2008/deuda/partenio.pdf.

Peebles, Gustav. 2010. "The Anthropology of Credit and Debt." *Annual Review of Anthropology,* 40: 225–40.

Pharo, Patrick. 2004. *Morale et sociologie: Le sens et les valeurs entre nature et culture.* Paris: Gallimard.

Pinheiro Machado, Rosana. 2010. "The Attribution of Authenticity to 'Real' and 'Fake' Branded Commodities in Brazil and China." In *Cultures of Commodity Branding,* ed. Andrew Bevan and David Wengrow, 109–29. Walnut Creek, CA: Left Coast Press.

———. 2011. *Made in China: (In)formalidade, pirataria e redes sociais na rota China-Paraguai-Brasil.* São Paulo: Hucitec Editora: ANPOCS.

Polanyi, Karl. 2001 [1944]. *The Great Transformation: The Political and Economic Origins of Our Time.* Boston: Beacon Press.

Poon, Martha. 2009. "From New Deal Institutions to Capital Markets: Commercial Consumer Risk Scores and the Making of Subprime Mortgage Finance." *Accounting, Organization and Society* 34: 654–74.

Prahalad, C. K. 2005. *The Fortune at the Bottom of the Pyramid: Eradicating Poverty through Profits.* Upper Saddle River, NJ: Wharton School Publishing.

Prevot Schapira, M.-F. 2002. "Buenos Aires en los años '90: Metropolización y desigualdades." *Revista EURE* 28 (85): 31–50.

Roig, Alexandre. 2009. "Separar de si, separar para si: Aproximaciones a las prácticas de ahorro domésticas en sectores populares urbanos argentinos." Paper presented at Latin American Sociological Association Conference, Río de Janeiro, Brazil.

Ruben, Oliven, and Rosana Pinheiro Machado. 2012. "From Country of the Future to Emergent Country: Popular Consumption in Brazil." In *Consumer Culture in Latin America,* ed. John Sinclair and Anna Cristina Pertierra, 53–66. New York: Palgrave Macmillan.

Sainz, Alfredo. 2009. *Negocios exitosos argentinos: Diez casos emblemáticos en la base de la pirámide social; Coto, Helados Pirulo, Marolio, La Salada, FIE Gran Poder, Calipso, Dr. Ahorro y más.* Buenos Aires: Planeta.

Salvatore, Ricardo. 1995. "Reformas de mercado y el lenguaje de la protesta popular." *Revista Sociedad* 7: 57–94.

Sauvadet, Thomas. 2006. "Le sentiment d'insécurité du 'dealer de cité.'" *Sociétés et jeunesses en difficulté,* no. 1 (Spring). https://sejed.revues.org/122 (accessed March 26, 2017).

Schorr, Martín. 2007. "La industria argentina entre 1976 y 1989: Cambios estructurales regresivos en una etapa de profundo replanteo del modo de acumulación local." *Papeles de Trabajo* 1: 1–53

Schuster, Caroline. 2015. *Social Collateral: Women and Microfinance in Paraguay's Smuggling Economy.* Berkeley: University of California Press.

Scott, James. 1976. *The Moral Economy of the Peasant: Rebellion and Subsistence in Southeast Asia.* New Haven, CT: Yale University Press.

Sigaud, Lygia. 2008. "Derecho y coerción moral en el mundo de los ingenios." *Crítica en Desarrollo: Revista Latinoamericana de Ciencias Sociales* 1: 81–107.

Simmel, Georg. 1900. *Philosophie des Geldes.* Leipzig: Duncker & Humbolt. Translated and edited by Tom Bottomore, David P. Frisby, and Kaethe Mengelberg as *The Philosophy of Money* (3rd enlarged ed., New York: Routledge, 2004).

Singerman, Diane. 1995. *Avenues of Participation: Family, Politics, and Networks in Urban Quarters of Cairo.* Princeton, NJ: Princeton University Press.

Singh, Supriya. 2013. *Globalization and Money: A Global South Perspective.* Lanham, MD: Rowman & Littlefield.

Stark, David, with Daniel Beunza, Monique Girard, and Janos Lukacs. 2009. *The Sense of Dissonance: Accounts of Worth in Economic Life.* Princeton, NJ: Princeton University Press.

Stoller, Paul. 2002. *Money Has No Smell: The Africanization of New York City.* Chicago: University of Chicago Press.

Strathern, Marilyn. 1999. *Property, Substance, and Effect: Anthropological Essays on Persons and Things.* New Brunswick, NJ: Athlone Press.

Suárez, Lourdes. 2006. "Inserción laboral de residentes en asentamientos precarios del Gran Buenos Aires: Orquestar la supervivencia atrapados en los barrios." *Estudios del Trabajo* 30: 67–94.

Thai, Hung Cam. 2014. *Insufficient Funds: The Culture of Money in Low-Wage Transnational Families.* Stanford, CA: Stanford University Press.

Théret, Bruno, ed. 2007. *La monnaie dévoilée par ses crises.* Paris: Éd. de l'EHESS.

———. 2008. "Les trois états de la monnaie: Approche interdisciplinaire du fait monétaire." *Revue Économique* 59 (4): 813–14.

Thompson, E. P. 1971. "The Moral Economy of the English Crowd in the Eighteenth Century." *Past & Present* 50: 76–136.

Tilly, Charles. 1999. "Power: Top Down and Bottom Up." *Journal of Political Philosophy* 7 (3): 330–52.

Torre, Juan Carlos. 1990. *La vieja guardia sindical y Peron: Sobre los orígenes del peronismo.* Buenos Aires: Editorial Sudamericana–Instituto Torcuato Di Tella.

———. 1998. *El proceso político de las reformas económicas en América Latina.* Buenos Aires: Paidos.

Torres, Horacio. 1975. "Evolución de los procesos de estructuración espacial urbana: El caso de Buenos Aires." *Desarrollo Económico: Revista de Ciencias Sociales* 15 (58): 281–306.

Van Schendel, Willem, and Itty Abraham. 2005. "Introduction: The Making of Illicitness." In *Illicit Flows and Criminal Things,* ed. van Schendel and Abraham, 1–37. Bloomington: Indiana University Press.

Venkatesh, Sudhir Alladi. 2008. *Off the Books: The Underground Economy of the Urban Poor.* Cambridge, MA: Harvard University Press.

Vommaro, Gabriel. 2010. "Regards croisés sur les rapports des classes populaires au politique en Argentine: Retour sur la question du 'clientélisme.'" PhD diss., École des hautes études en sciences sociales.

Wacquant, Loïc. 2002. "Scrutinizing the Street: Poverty, Morality, and the Pitfalls of Urban Ethnography." *American Journal of Sociology* 107: 1468–1532.

———. 2008. *Urban Outcasts: A Comparative Sociology of Advanced Marginality.* Malden, MA: Polity Press.

Weber, Florence. 2005. *Le sang, le nom, le quotidien: Une sociologie de la parenté pratique.* Paris: Aux lieux d'être.

Weber, Max. 1991 [1946]. *From Max Weber: Essays in Sociology.* Edited and translated by H. H. Gerth and C. Wright Mills. New York: Routledge, 1991.

———. 2001 [1904–5]. *The Protestant Ethic and the Spirit of Capitalism.* New York: Routledge.

———. 2013 [1922]. *Economy and Society: An Outline of Interpretive Sociology.* Translated by Ephraim Fischoff et al. Edited by Guenther Roth and Claus Wittich. 2 vols. Berkeley: University of California Press.

Weiner, Annette B. 1992. *Inalienable Possessions: The Paradox of Keeping-While-Giving.* Berkeley: University of California Press.

Wherry, Frederick F. 2008. "The Social Characterizations of Price: The Fool, the Faithful, the Frivolous, and the Frugal." *Sociological Theory* 26: 363–79.

———. 2012. *The Culture of Markets.* Malden, MA: Polity Press.

———. 2016. "Relational Accounting: A Cultural Approach." *American Journal of Cultural Sociology* 4 (2): 131–56, doi:10.1057/ajcs.2016.1.

White, W. F. 1973. *Street Corner Society.* Chicago: University of Chicago Press.

Wilkis, Ariel. 2013. *Las sospechas del dinero: Moral y economía en el mundo popular.* Buenos Aires: Paidos.

———. 2014. "Sociología del credito y economía de las clases populares." *Revista Mexicana de Sociología* 76: 225–52.

Woods, Marcela. 2009. "Instituciones de la sociedad civil y dominación estatal: Efectos de despolitización de la intervención social de la Iglesia Católica." In *Estado y movimientos sociales: Estudios etnográficos en Argentina y Brasil,* ed. Mabel Grimberg, María Ines Fernández Alvarez, and Marcelo Rosa, 113–29. Buenos Aires: Editorial Antropofagia.

Zaloom, Caitlin. 2012. "Traders." In *The Oxford Handbook of the Sociology of Finance,* ed. Karin Knorr-Cetina and Alex Preda, 169–86. Oxford: Oxford University Press.

Zapata, Laura. 2005. *La mano que acaricia la pobreza: Etnografía del voluntariado católico.* Buenos Aires: Editorial Antropofagia.

Zelizer, Viviana A. 1994. *The Social Meaning of Money: Pin Money, Paychecks, Poor Relief, and Other Currencies.* Princeton, NJ: Princeton University Press.

———. 1996. " Payments and Social Ties." *Sociological Forum* 11 (3): 481–95.

———. 2005. *The Purchase of Intimacy.* Princeton, NJ: Princeton University Press.

———. 2010. "Circuits in Economic Life." In *Economic Lives: How Culture Shapes the Economy,* ed. Zelizer, 344–54. Princeton, NJ: Princeton University Press.

———. 2012. "How I Became a Relational Economic Sociologist and What Does That Mean?" *Politics & Society* 40: 145–74.

———. 2016. "My Money Obsession." www.booksandideas.net/Twenty-Years-After-The-Social-Meaning-of-Money.html (accessed March 26, 2017).

Zuleta Puceiro, Enrique, et al. 1990. "Modelos de partido político y su financiamiento." *Boletín informativo techint,* no. 264 (September–December): 41–71.

Index

CULTURE AND ECONOMIC LIFE

Diverse sets of actors create meaning in markets: consumers and socially engaged actors from below; producers, suppliers, and distributors from above; and the gatekeepers and intermediaries that span these levels. Scholars have studied the interactions of people, objects, and technology; charted networks of innovation and diffusion among producers and consumers; and explored the categories that constrain and enable economic action. This series captures the many angles in which these phenomena have been investigated and serves as a high-profile forum for discussing the evolution, creation, and consequences of commerce and culture.

Artistic Values: How Artists Make the Things They Do Worth Doing
Alison Gerber
2017

Behind the Laughs: Community and Inequality in Comedy
Michael P. Jeffries
2017

Freedom from Work: Embracing Financial Self-Help
in the United States and Argentina
Daniel Fridman
2016